World of Dance

European Dance

Robin Rinaldi

CHELSEA HOUSE
P U B L I S H E R S
A Haights Cross Communications Company
Philadelphia

Frontispiece: A group of Romanie Gypsies, circa 1850, dance around a campfire performing the *quadrille*. A French ballroom dance, the *quadrille* became popular throughout Europe in the nineteenth century.

CHELSEA HOUSE PUBLISHERS
VP, NEW PRODUCT DEVELOPMENT Sally Cheney
DIRECTOR OF PRODUCTION Kim Shinners
CREATIVE MANAGER Takeshi Takahashi
MANUFACTURING MANAGER Diann Grasse

Staff for EUROPEAN DANCE
EDITOR Ben Kim
PRODUCTION EDITOR Megan Emery
PICTURE RESEARCHER Pat Holl
SERIES & COVER DESIGNER Terry Mallon
LAYOUT 21st Century Publishing and Communications, Inc.

A Haights Cross Communications ⚔ Company

www.chelseahouse.com

First Printing

1 3 5 7 9 8 6 4 2

Library of Congress Cataloging-in-Publication Data

Rinaldi, Robin.
  European dance: Ireland, Poland, & Spain / by Robin Rinaldi.
    p. cm. — (World of dance)
Summary: Introduces the history, methods of teaching, ceremonial
styles, basic steps, and famous figures of traditional Irish, Polish,
and Spanish dance. Includes bibliographical references and index.
  ISBN 0-7910-7643-1 (hardcover) — ISBN 0-7910-7778-0 (pbk.) 1.
Dance—Europe—Juvenile literature. [1. Dance—Europe. 2. Folk
dancing.] I. Title. II. Series. GV1643.R56 2004 793.3'094—dc22
                                                    2003023054

Table of Contents

Introduction

Elizabeth A. Hanley
Associate Professor of Kinesiology, Penn State University

Dance has existed from time immemorial. It has been an integral part of celebrations and rituals, a means of communication with gods and among humans, and a basic source of enjoyment and beauty.

Dance is a fundamental element of human behavior and has evolved over the years from primitive movement of the earliest civilizations to traditional ethnic or folk styles, to the classical ballet and modern dance genres popular today. The term 'dance' is a broad one and, therefore, is not limited to the genres noted above. In the twenty-first century, dance includes ballroom, jazz, tap, aerobics, and a myriad of other movement activities.

The richness of cultural traditions observed in the ethnic, or folk, dance genre offers the participant, as well as the spectator, insight into the customs, geography, dress, and religious nature of a particular people. Originally passed on from one generation to the next, many ethnic, or folk, dances continue to evolve as our civilization and society change. From these quaint beginnings of traditional dance, a new genre emerged as a way to appeal to the upper level of society: ballet. This new form of dance rose quickly in popularity and remains so today. The genre of ethnic, or folk, dance continues to be an important part of ethnic communities throughout the United States, particularly in large cities.

When the era of modern dance emerged as a contrast and a challenge to the rigorously structured world of ballet, it was not readily accepted as an art form. Modern dance was interested in the communication of emotional experiences—through basic movement, through uninhibited movement—not through the academic tradition of ballet masters. Modern dance, however, found its aficionados and is a popular art form today.

No dance form is permanent, definitive, or ultimate. Change occurs, but the basic element of dance endures. Dance is for all people. One need only recall that dance needs neither common race nor common language for communication; it has been a universal means of communication forever.

The WORLD OF DANCE series provides a starting point for readers interested in learning about ethnic, or folk, dances of world cultures, as well as the art forms of ballet and modern dance. This series will feature an overview of the development of these dance genres, from a historical perspective to a practical one. Highlighting specific cultures, their dance steps and movements, and their customs and traditions will underscore the importance of these fundamental elements for the reader. Ballet and modern dance, more recent artistic dance genres, are explored in detail as well, giving the reader a comprehensive knowledge of their past, present, and potential future.

The one fact that each reader should remember is that dance has always been, and always will be, a form of communication. This is its legacy to the world.

In this volume, Robin Rinaldi will examine three countries—Ireland, Poland, and Spain—that have had a major impact on both European and, in a larger sense, Western dance. With the development of the *reel* and *jig*, among others, Ireland has a rich celebratory dance tradition that has laid the foundation for today's popular step dances such as *Riverdance* and *Lord of Dance*.

Poland, despite its tumultuous history, also developed an identity through its dance tradition. Such dances as the *mazur* and *polonez*, which appeared in ballrooms throughout Europe in the eighteenth and nineteenth centuries, gave Poland a semblance of being that it sorely needed.

Spain, too, was affected by a number of outside influences but developed many unique forms of dance, such as *flamenco* and *bolero*, that emphasized free movements of both the arms and legs, and thrived in a time when the rest of Europe was enthralled with classic ballet.

Foreword

Jacques D'Amboise
Founder, National Dance Institute

"In song and dance, man expresses himself as a member of a higher community. He has forgotten how to walk and speak and is on the way into flying into the air, dancing . . . his very gestures express enchantment."

—Friedrich Nietzsche

On Maria Dancing by Robert Burns
How graceful Maria leads the dance!
She's life itself. I never saw a foot
So nimble and so elegant; it speaks,
And the sweet whispering poetry it makes
Shames the musicians.

In a conversation with Balanchine discussing the definition of dance, we evolved the following description: "Dance is an expression of time and space, using the control of movement and gesture to communicate."

Dance is central to the human being's expression of emotion. Every time we shake someone's hand, lift a glass in a toast, wave goodbye, or applaud a performer—we are doing a form of dance. We live in a universe of time and space, and dance is an art form invented by human beings to express and convey emotions. Dance is profound.

There are melodies that, when played, will cause your heart to droop with sadness for no known reason. Or a rousing jig or mazurka will have your foot tapping in an accompanying rhythm, seemingly beyond your control. The emotions, contacted through music, spur the body to react physically. Our bodies have just been programmed to express emotions. We dance for many reasons: for religious rituals from the most ancient times; for dealing with sadness, tearfully swaying and holding hands at

8

wake; for celebrating weddings, joyfully spinning in circles; for entertainment; for dating and mating. How many millions of couples through the ages have said, "We met at a dance?" But most of all, we dance for joy, often exclaiming, "How I love to dance!" Oh, the JOY OF DANCE!!

I was teaching dance at a boarding school for emotionally disturbed children, ages 9 through 16. They were participating with 20 other schools in the National Dance Institute's (NDI) year-round program. The boarding school children had been traumatized in frightening and mind-boggling ways. There were a dozen students in my class, and the average attention span may have been 15 seconds—which made for a raucous bunch. This was a tough class.

One young boy, an 11-year-old, was an exception. He never took his eyes off of me for the 35 minutes of the dance class, and they were blazing blue eyes—electric, set in a chalk white face. His body was slim, trim, superbly proportioned, and he stood arrow-straight. His lips were clamped in a rigid, determined line as he learned and executed every dance step with amazing skill. His concentration was intense despite the wild cavorting, noise, and otherwise disruptive behavior supplied by his fellow classmates.

At the end of class I went up to him and said, "Wow, can you dance. You're great! What's your name?"

Those blue eyes didn't blink. Then he parted his ridged lips and bared his teeth in a grimace that may have been a smile. He had a big hole where his front teeth should be. I covered my shock and didn't let it show. Both top and bottom incisors had been worn away by his continual grinding and rubbing of them together. One of the supervisors of the school rushed over to me and said, "Oh, his name is Michael. He's very intelligent but he doesn't speak."

I heard Michael's story from the supervisor. Apparently, when he was a toddler in his playpen, he witnessed his father shooting his mother, then putting the gun to his own head, the father killed himself. It was close to three days before the neighbors broke in to find the dead and swollen bodies of his parents. The dehydrated and starving little boy was stuck in his playpen, sitting in his own filth. The orphaned Michael disappeared into the foster care system, eventually ending up in the boarding school. No one had ever heard him speak.

In the ensuing weeks of dance class, I built and developed choreography for Michael and his classmates. In the spring, they were scheduled to dance in a spectacular NDI show called *The Event of the Year*. At the boarding school, I used Michael as the leader and as a model for the others and began welding all of the kids together, inventing a vigorous and energetic dance to utilize their explosive energy. It took a while, but they were coming together, little by little over the months. And through all that time, the best in the class—the determined and concentrating Michael—never spoke.

That spring, dancers from the 22 different schools with which the NDI had dance programs were scheduled to come together at Madison Square Garden for *The Event of the Year*. There would be over 2,000 dancers, a symphony orchestra, a jazz orchestra, a chorus, Broadway stars, narrators, and Native American Indian drummers. There was scenery that was the length of an entire city block and visiting guest children from six foreign countries coming to dance with our New York City children. All of these elements had to come together and fit into a spectacular performance, with only one day of rehearsal. The foremost challenge was how to get 2,000 dancing children on stage for the opening number.

At NDI, we have developed a system called "The Runs." First, we divide the stage into a grid with colored lines making the outlines of box shapes, making a mosaic of patterns and shapes on the stage floor. Each outlined box holds a class from one of the schools, which would consist of 15 to 30 children. Then, we add various colored lines as tracks, starting offstage and leading to the boxes. The dancers line up in the wings, hallways, and various holding areas on either side of the stage. At the end of the overture, they burst onto stage, running and leaping and following their colored tracks to their respective boxes, where they explode into the opening dance number.

We had less than three minutes to accomplish "The Runs." It's as if a couple of dozen trains coming from different places and traveling on different tracks all arrived at a station at the same time, safely pulling into their allotted spaces. But even before starting, it would take us almost an hour just to get the dancers lined up in the correct holding areas offstage, ready to make their entrance. We had scheduled one shot to rehearse the opening. It had to work the first time or we would have to repeat everything. That meant going into overtime at a great expense.

I gave the cue to start the number. The orchestra, singers, lights, and stagehands all commenced on cue, and the avalanche of 2,000 children were let loose on their tracks. "The Runs" had begun!

After about a minute, I realized something was wrong. There was a big pileup on stage left and children were colliding into each other and bunching up behind some obstacle. I ran over to discover the source of the problem—Michael and his classmates. He had ignored everything and led the group from his school right up front, as close to the audience as he could get. Inspiring his dancing buddies, they were a crew of leaping, contorting demons—dancing up a storm, but blocking some 600 other dancers trying to get through.

I rushed up to them yelling, "You're in the wrong place! Back up! Back up!"

Michael—with his eyes blazing, mouth open, and legs and arms spinning in dance movements like an eggbeater—yelled out, "Oh, I am so happy! I am so happy! Thank you Jacques! Oh, it's so good! I am so happy!"

I backed off, stunned into silence. I sat down in the first row of the audience to be joined by several of the supervisors, teachers, and chaperones from Michael's school, our mouths open in wonder. The spirit of dance had taken over Michael and his classmates. No one danced better or with more passion in the whole show that night and with Michael leading the way—the JOY OF DANCE at work. (We went into overtime but so what!)

1

The Roots of
Irish Dancing

Ireland is an island, about the size of West Virginia, off the
western coast of England. The southern part of the island
consists of twenty-six counties that make up the Irish Republic,
while the northern tip contains six counties known as Northern
Ireland. Northern Ireland, whose population is mostly Protestant, is part of the United Kingdom—which also includes
England, Scotland, and Wales—while the predominantly
Catholic Irish Republic is a separate, sovereign nation.

Regardless of the distinct identities and national statuses of
Northern Ireland and the Irish Republic, and the political and
religious strife that has separated the two in the twentieth
century, the Irish people all share a common ethnicity,
language, and culture. To say that Ireland's long and colorful
history, which can be traced back to 7000 B.C., has influenced
its traditional dances is an understatement—it has influenced most of European and Western civilization in general.

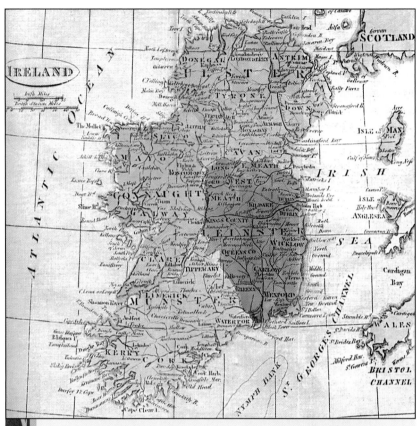

Ireland, shown here in 1808, has had a profound effect on Western dance, supplying such movements as the *jig, hornpipe,* and *reel.*

CELTS AND CHRISTIANS

The Irish people are descendents of the ancient Celts (kelts), a tribe who settled in what is now France, Spain, and England about five hundred years before Jesus Christ, and who arrived in Ireland about 350 B.C. Known as great warriors who rushed to battle naked, wearing only sandals and golden neck ornaments, the Celts also possessed a rich pagan culture. They worshipped a variety of gods and goddesses as well as nature itself, especially in the form of sacred trees such as oaks. In all the other present-day countries they inhabited, the Celts were

13

absorbed into subsequent tribes and nations; Ireland remains the only Celtic nation that has survived to the present.

Celtic dances of this time would have centered around various rituals: the worship of trees, the psychological preparation for war, courtships and marriages, and the changing of the seasons. The latter types of celebrations survived well into the nineteenth century and included dancing round bonfires on Beltane (May 1) to mark the coming warmth of summer, and on Samhain or All Hallow's Eve (October 31) to honor the dead and prepare for winter.

The advent of Christianity had a marked impact on Ireland. After an escaped Roman slave named Patricius—later known as St. Patrick—arrived in Ireland in 432 A.D. with his message of Christian salvation, Ireland evolved into a Catholic enclave from which monks and scholars preserved much of European history during the barbarous times known as the Dark and Middle Ages (500–1200 A.D.). And though the names of the Celtic feasts, and their purported meanings, changed— from Beltane to May Day and from Samhain to All Saints' Day, for example—many of the actual pagan rituals remained.

THE ANGLO-NORMAN INFLUENCE

From about 800 A.D. onward, Ireland withstood several invasions, starting with the Viking, who settled the first Irish towns including the city of Dublin. The Anglo-Normans, who today we would recognize as French, English, and Welsh, followed in 1169 A.D., beginning a long period of English rule in Ireland. The Anglo-Normans brought with them *round dances*, simple circular dances in which the participants linked arms or held hands while moving in a circle, usually counterclockwise. These dances could be performed around a tree or bonfire, and a few of them survive today. They are still danced on June 20—the Christian feast of St. John's Day and the pagan celebration of the summer solstice.

During the 1500s, visitors to Ireland made mention of the

rince fada, or *long dance*, which consists of a row of men facing a row of women. Beginning at one end of the line, the couples start dancing one by one until all have joined in. One account of a long dance describes how all the social classes took part in the rince fada together, "one after another of all conditions, the masters, mistresses and servants."[1]

This observation typifies one of the symbolic functions of *folk dance*, which is to solidify a group's identity, whether that group is a social class, a town, or an entire nation. In this case, the mingling of all the classes communicated a nonverbal message that, beneath superficial social distinctions, the rural Irish shared a common bond.

Another early Irish dance, imported from France via England and Scotland, was called the *hey*, a serpentine arrangement in which several men and women passed each other shoulder to shoulder, weaving between one another or alternately tracing a figure-eight on the floor. The hey also served a symbolic function. The chain configuration that dancers created as they passed represented the "great chain of being" or the underlying natural order of the universe. Later on, when the hey, like many other folk dances, was adapted to the ballrooms of Renaissance Europe, it frequently was the final dance of the evening, lending an endnote of harmony and order to the proceedings.

THE CHURCH DISAPPROVES

As first the Catholic, and then, beginning in the 1600s, also the Protestant churches took power in Ireland, traditional dances became less focused on religious ritual and feeling. Throughout much of Christianity's history, church leaders portrayed music as high art that pleased God, giving it a place in the liturgy and sponsoring musical composition in both religious and secular environments. By contrast, the Christian church of the seventeenth century considered dancing a trivial entertainment at best—and as a potentially sinful pastime at worst, whereby young men and women might enjoy too much physical contact.

And yet Irish people continued to celebrate both spiritual and nonspiritual occasions with dancing. They danced at weddings, fairs, and harvest festivals. They also danced on holy days and every Sunday, usually to the accompaniment of a piper or fiddler. As author Richard Head described it in 1620: "Their Sunday is the most leisure day they have in which they use all manner of sport; in every field a fiddle and the lasses footing it till they are all of a foam." [2]

The Irish also engaged in *withy dances*, in which dancers encircled fires while holding twigs between them, and *sword dances*, in which several men connected their swords—or wooden sticks—in a close circle, a ritual possibly left over from early war dances.

Each Irish town has its own patron saint with an annual feast day, or "pattern," set aside for the saint. During patterns, the parishioners' custom was to meet near the local alehouse in the afternoon for a *cake dance*, in which a huge cake adorned with flowers and fruit was brought out on a round board placed high in the center of a circle. To the accompaniment of a piper, the villagers danced around the cake in a sort of marathon. The last couple dancing after the others had given up from fatigue would win the prize, or "take the cake."

The exact movements of cake dances, sword dances, and many others aren't known for sure. That's because folk dancing by its very nature is difficult to record; it originated with rural, often illiterate people and was passed down (and changed) from person to person, without being written or recorded in any way. Also, unlike music, which consists of a finite number of notes and thus can eventually be scored, the variety of human dance movements is virtually endless, with steps often improvised. For these reasons, we have only a sketchy view of the early dances mentioned above, many of which are no longer performed in their original form or context.

As part of their naval training, British cadets practice one of Ireland's oldest dances, the *hornpipe*, which features complex, nimble footwork. The dance originated in Scotland and Wales where it was associated with the rituals of the harvest and springtime fertility celebrations.

SURVIVING IRISH DANCES

Fortunately, some dances from as far back as the 1600s have survived to the present day. Foremost among these is the *hornpipe*, a step dance popular not only in Ireland but England and Scotland, which emphasizes leg action and the beating out of rhythms with the feet in time to the music. The name comes from a reed pipe, often made of animal horns and skins, played by shepherds, and it describes not only a dance but also the type of music that accompanies it, whose timing has varied over the years. One example of hornpipe music in its fully orchestrated form is George Frederic Handel's *Water Music*, Nos. 9 and 12. But for folk dancing purposes, a more rugged, homemade style of music was played for the hornpipe.

Another early dance that still enjoys great popularity is the *reel*. Perhaps the most common type of dance in Ireland, its name comes from the Anglo word *hreol*, which means to make a weaving motion, and that's exactly what the earliest reels did. Much like the hey, the first reels, believed to have originated in Scotland, featured three or four dancers beginning in a straight line, then weaving around one another in a figure-eight pattern; in fact the "hey" pattern became so common that the hey eventually became known as one of many types of reels.

By the end of the eighteenth century, Irish people were dancing reels, hornpipes, long dances, and innumerable other formations for occasions as celebratory as Christmas and as

THE HORNPIPE

In its original form, the hornpipe was danced in Scotland and Wales by shepherds while they accompanied themselves on their reed pipes of the same name—hence the emphasis on the legs and feet since the men's hands were occupied by their instruments. The dance is also associated with the rituals of the harvest and with springtime fertility celebrations, as its Gaelic word, *cornphiopa*, refers to the cornucopia or horn of plenty, a symbol of food and abundance.

The hornpipe could also be danced by couples and in the figure of a long dance, but in Ireland it was primarily performed as a solo dance not only at seasonal feasts but also at wakes and in alehouses on Saturday nights. Both men and women, wearing either clogs or hard shoes, would take turns tapping out a fiddler's rhythm on a wooden board or even an unhinged door placed on the floor. In lieu of a board, the tabletops of the alehouse sufficed.

mundane as a day of rest from working. The Catholic Church still vehemently disapproved, with one priest writing that "women dancers are the cause of many evils, because it is they who bear arms in the devil's army."[3] Another priest went so far as to violently beat a piper he found playing for a dance.

This seemed to have little effect on the deeply religious but unabashedly good-natured Irish villagers, who saw no conflict in maintaining their earthy, pagan customs. Thus in 1787, though the church had been established in Ireland for well over 1,200 years, a traveler writes an account of a May Day celebration harkening back to the ancient rites of Beltane in which twenty-four couples, dressed in white with ribbons hanging from their clothes, danced over a space a quarter-mile long; on one end a maypole and on the other end a bonfire.

Starting in the late 1700s the hornpipe became closely associated with sailors of Britain's Royal Navy, also called "jolly tars." From this reference comes the name of the most well-known version, the "Sailor's Hornpipe" or the "Jacky Tar," which features extremely nimble foot movements and changes of balance. Sailors on board ships were said to perform the popular dance whenever possible, and in the 1800s the dance was even formally included in naval training curriculum. It was by no means restricted to sailors and remained a favorite in rural Ireland as well as at fashionable London balls.

Today in Ireland, two types of hornpipes prevail: a single is a graceful women's dance using shuffles and light taps, while a double, performed by men, utilizes much harder, more grinding steps of great difficulty. The hornpipe, though similar to other step dances such as the reel and jig, is often danced to a slower tempo, allowing much more complex steps and often very high kicks.

THE REEL

Arguably the most common and popular dance in Ireland, the reel takes many variations. Its earliest form was a group dance in which the participants made weaving, chaining, and linking patterns such as figure-eights around each other. In between these shifts of their positions on the floor, the dancers would unlink and improvise step dances—the quick-footed legwork that is also characteristic of the jig and hornpipe—so that the reel alternated between intricate individual footwork and interweaving group figures, becoming a pattern within a pattern.

Group reels are classified by the number of participants: for instance, "three-hand" reels are for three dancers. They can include anywhere from two to sixteen dancers. Four-hand reels, also known as *Scotch reels*, in which two couples face each other throughout the dance, may have been the precursor to American square dancing. Six-hand reels later became popular in the United States as *Virginia reels*. The word "reel" also defines the type of quick music that first accompanied these dances, but the music and steps are now interchangeable so that jigs can be danced to reel-time music and vice versa.

Group reels are danced in England and Scotland as well as Ireland, but only in Ireland does the term "reel" refer quite commonly to solo step dances to reel-time music. There are three types of solo reels:

- The single reel is fast in tempo, but its footwork is simple, so it's often used to teach novices the basics of step dancing. It is performed in soft shoes.

- The double reel (not to be confused with a two-hand reel or couple's reel) is most common. Also performed in soft shoes, it has a slower tempo but much more complex footwork involving continual drumming of the heel and toe known as "batters."

- The treble reel, danced in hard shoes, is rarely performed, even in competitive dancing and is staged almost exclusively by modern Irish dance troupes, such as *Riverdance* and *Lord of the Dance.*

In the *Scotch reel*, or four-hand reel, two couples alternate footwork with weaving patterns. It may be the precursor to American square dancing and is one of several reels, which is Ireland's most popular dance.

2

The Development of Modern Irish Dancing

Up until about the 1750s, traditional dancing had developed quite organically in the fields and villages of Ireland. It evolved out of rituals associated with nature, farming, rites of passage, and religion. Ireland exported its own lexicon of steps to neighboring countries such as Scotland, England, and France, and in return it took the practices of these neighbors and made them its own.

This evolution and exchange of movement is typical of folk dancing, which, like language, is always changing depending on people's needs and customs, and spreading beyond the borders of its origin. Thus the reel, which probably originated in Scotland, was by this time one of the most popular Irish dances, and the *jig*, a lively step dance which most people associate with Ireland, played a large part in the tradition of England's *morris dance*—a ceremonial dance performed by two long columns of men—which in turn had migrated north from Spain in the twelfth century.

The *morris dance* originated in medieval Spain, migrated to Great Britain, and is still performed today by two long columns of men as a ceremonial dance.

But in the eighteenth century, Ireland's traditional dances were about to undergo a vital period of expansion, standardization, and popularity, due in large part to dancing masters who roamed the country and shared their love of Irish dance.

THE DANCING MASTERS

At some point in the 1700s, certain Irish men set out to teach their countrymen how to dance. Though no one is quite sure who the first Irish dancing master was or what motivated these men to take on such an occupation, we can guess that by this time dancing had become so important to the Irish that many of them wanted to be sure to learn all the customary *social dances* and also teach them to their children.

The dancing master was a somewhat colorful figure in Irish history. Carrying a cane and dressed in hat and pumps (in a countryside where most villagers barely had a decent pair of shoes), he had no house of his own but roamed his territory with a piper or fiddler, staying as a guest in the homes of farmers. For several weeks at a time, the dancing master would hold classes in a barn; each pupil earning him about sixpence, which he shared with the musician. Villagers eagerly awaited the arrival of a dancing master and happily put him up, as it heralded several weeks' worth of dancing and fiddling for everyone.

The dancing masters taught a great deal to their students. First and foremost, they codified the practice of *step dancing*, which forms the basis of most Irish dance. Step dancing is a general term for the nimble footwork, performed in place with the hands at the sides, which modern viewers associate with Irish dancing. It consists of several small, quick foot movements such as *shuffles*, *cuts*, and *batters*, as well as hopping patterns like the side step and rising step. Step dances can be done in hard-soled shoes so that the movements are loud and percussive, much like a tap dance, or they can be done in soft shoes that make no noise and give a lighter, almost airborne impression. Either way, the dancer is expected to move in perfect time to the music, beating out its rhythm with his or her feet.

The first steps a dancing master taught his students were usually the side step, used in the reel, and the rising step, used in the jig. In order to teach Irish children the difference between their right and left foot, especially if the teacher was facing the students and thus dancing on the opposite foot, he would tie a piece of straw to their right foot and a piece of hay to their left. Though some dancing masters included girls in their classes, they generally taught them the lighter, soft-shoe steps and reserved the heavier, percussive dances for the boys. And though the dance lessons tended to cross social and economic classes, including anyone who could afford the six-pence fee, the masters did try to impart an air of refinement and grace to the proceedings. To this end, many think it was the dancing masters who standardized the practice of keeping the arms stationary at the side of the body, which they achieved by placing heavy stones in the students' hands as they danced. Others say the Irish's straight arms were an inventive way to get around the church's prohibitions against dancing, which it defined as moving the legs *and arms* to music.

The dancing masters are thus credited with imparting to Irish youngsters the training needed for the longstanding tradition of *solo step dancing*, which continues to this day worldwide in formal competitions, local pubs, and professional touring troupes such as *Riverdance* and *Lord of the Dance.*

THE FIRST CEILIS AND SET DANCES

Of course, not every student could master the difficult foot-work involved in the solo jig, reel, and hornpipe. Then, too, everyone in the village wanted to dance together—young and old, men and women, boys and girls; so the dancing masters had to teach some group dances, which were easier to learn and more communal. These early social dances were usually held at someone's home or barn, or outdoors at a crossroads on Sunday evenings. A dance of this kind was called a *ceili* (kaylee) which translates to "an evening chat or gathering," or *ceilithe* for plural.

Today the dancing masters are recognized as the origina-tors of a number of Irish social dances called ceili dances. All these dances use the same basic steps but have dancers move in a circular, square, or long-line pattern, often in male-female couplings that switch off throughout the course of the dance, allowing everyone a chance to dance with everyone else. The popular ceili dances, invented by the dancing masters, bear regional and folksy names such as "The Siege of Ennis," "The Walls of Limerick," and "The Haymaker's Jig." All a student had to do was learn the five basic steps—

IRISH STEPS

A ceili dance isn't difficult to do once you know the five basic steps. All ceili dances use combinations of these steps with the hands either down at the sides, or held about shoulder height with bent elbows that are latched onto a partner, or linked in a chain. All the steps are done on the balls of the feet.

- The *side step* is also the basic step of the reel. It begins with the feet together: (1) hop lightly onto the left foot as the right knee bends and the right foot lifts slightly off the floor; (2) step to the right; (3) close the left foot behind the right, transferring the weight to the left; (4) step again to the right; (5) close the left foot again in the same way; (6) step to the right; (7) close the left foot again, transferring the weight to the left and letting the right knee bend slightly and the foot come off the floor.

- *Two short threes* begins where the side step leaves off, with the weight on the ball of the left foot and the right foot slightly off the floor: (and 1) hop on the left foot while sweeping the right foot quickly behind the left by bending the right knee, then step back onto the right foot and let the left come off the ground; (2) step on the left, lifting the right in back; (3) step on the right, letting the left come up a bit in front; (and 4) hop on the right foot while sweeping the left foot quickly behind the right by bending the left knee, then step back onto the left foot and let the right come off the ground; (5) step onto the right, lifting the left in back; (6) step on the left, letting the right come up a bit in front.

the rising step, side step, promenade, two short threes, and the sink and grind—and then follow the floor pattern in order to participate in a ceili.

- The *promenade* is similar to the side step but shorter, with only four counts instead of seven. Beginning with the feet together: (1) hop lightly on the left while bending the right knee and letting the right foot come off the ground; (2) step forward on the right; (3) close the left foot behind the right and step on it; (4) step onto the right and raise the left foot behind it. Then repeat the sequence on the other leg, beginning by hopping onto the right.

- The *rising step* is also the basic step of the jig: (1) hop on the left foot, bending the right knee and lifting the right foot in front; (2) hop again on the left, quickly sweeping the bent right foot to the back of the left knee; (3) step back on the right; (4) Now hop on the right, quickly sweeping the left foot behind the right; (5) step back onto the left; (6) step front onto the right; (7) bring left foot behind right and step onto it, letting the right raise off the floor; (8) step onto the right.

- The *sink* and *grind* is also used in the jig: (1) jump onto the balls of both feet at once, the right in front of the left; (2) hop on the left, letting the right raise up in front; (3) hop again on the left, sweeping the right quickly behind the left with bent knee; (4) step back onto the right letting the left leg lift a bit off the ground; (5) step onto the left; (6) bring right foot behind left, sinking into the whole foot while letting the left leg lift a little off the ground; (7) step onto the left.

The most widely known Irish dance, the *jig* can be performed solo, in couples, or in groups and is a fast step dance known for its lively movement of the feet and legs.

But the dancing masters weren't done yet. In addition to the solo dances and the ceili dances, various foreign dances from the ballrooms of Europe were making their way to Ireland's shores via its many ports and travelers, and through the influence of British rule. During the eighteenth and nineteenth centuries, for example, the *quadrille* from France, the *waltz* from Austria, and the *scottische* from Germany all found their way to rural Ireland and into the dancing masters' classes, where they were given local flavor and a dash of Irish step dancing, and then added to the traditional repertoire. These originally foreign dances were called *set dances, country dances,* or *country sets.* The popularity of these dances was astounding: By 1728, one dancing master had published more than 900 country dances, all of which involved groups of dancers moving in circles, lines, or squares.

By far the most popular, and later on the most controversial, of these imported dances was the French quadrille, a dance for four couples who face each other in a square, change places and then trace the square figure by a series of walking and sliding steps. In the ballrooms of France, the quadrille was a stately—some would even say boring— affair in which couples basically walked from one formation to another. Once the dance arrived in the Irish countryside it was given livelier footwork and a faster tempo. Thus the French "set of quadrilles" became known simply to the Irish as a *set*, or when only two couples were involved, a *half-set.*

THE GAELIC LEAGUE

Though the British ruled Irish soil for almost eight centuries— from 1169 to 1921 when the southern Irish counties formed the Irish Republic—the Irish people continually struggled to retain their own Celtic language, culture, and customs. After the Great Potato Famine of the 1840s decimated the Irish population—killing a million and a half people and forcing a million more to move to America and Australia in a desperate flight from poverty and illness—Irish dancing understandably stagnated. For many decades people had to concern themselves with survival.

But the resilient Irish spirit bounced back in 1893 in the form of the Gaelic League, a commission founded in Dublin with the goal of reviving and preserving Celtic language and culture. In 1897, the London branch of the Gaelic League organized the first formal ceili, taking the dances once performed in barns and at crossroads and moving them inside large urban halls. These first ceilithe featured traditional dances such as the double jig along with current European ones like the waltz and quadrille,

THE JIG

The dance most associated with Ireland, the jig is a fast step dance in which the legs and feet perform lively, sometimes virtuosic movements while the body moves straight up and down. Although often performed as a vigorous solo that highlights the dancer's strength and rhythm, the jig can also be done as a group or with couples. The jig also refers to a type of Irish song. As a result, many Irish dances that don't actually utilize jig steps are loosely called "jigs" only because their accompanying music is in jig-time. One popular example is the group dance called the *Haymaker's Jig*. Confusing the issue further is the fact that not only is the jig closely related to the hornpipe and reel, but these three terms have sometimes been used interchangeably. Like other step dances, the jig employs shuffles, batters, and hops; its most basic step is called the rising step. In addition to the basic jig, there are several jig variations:

and the idea quickly spread back to Ireland and throughout the Irish diasporas worldwide.

But with the Irish still under great political, economic, and cultural pressures, the content of the ceilithe, which the Gaelic League soon began publishing, became a lightning rod for debate over dances that were "truly Irish" versus those that were "foreign." The quadrilles in particular, which proved quite popular, came under fierce attack. It seems the Irish were torn between the urge to keep their native traditions intact while also upgrading the sometimes crude image the rest of Europe—Great Britain in particular—had of them. Many members of the Gaelic League wanted to keep the foreign dances on the basis of their refinement and popularity, while

- The single jig, danced a bit faster than a regular jig, is a light dance that employs aerial steps and is performed in soft shoes.

- The slip jig, also called the hop jig, is performed mostly by young girls. It, too, is a fast, light, soft-shoe dance in which the girl travels the floor using graceful hopping steps, often balancing very high on her toes.

- The double jig is mostly a dance for men, so named because of its double batters and shuffles. It can be danced in soft or hard shoes, and when danced in hard shoes it's sometimes called a treble jig or heavy jig.

The jig has been danced in Ireland since at least the 1600s and was uniformly taught as a foundation by the dancing masters of the 1800s. Today the jig is performed at Irish social dances and competitions, and virtuosic examples of the slip jig and treble jig can be seen in popular Irish dancing shows.

The *quadrille*, which came from the ballrooms of France, was one of the most popular dances in nineteenth-century Europe. Once transported to Ireland, it ignited controversy over native versus foreign customs.

others, such as this anonymous writer in a 1904 article in *Western People* newspaper, balked:

"Just fancy learning Irish dancing from books, and worse still from books inspired in London! Faugh! The thing is impossible . . ."[4]

One reason it can be difficult to distinguish whether the

debated dances were actually of "high" or "low" origin, and exactly how "native" or "foreign" they were, is because folk dance is not only continually evolving and migrating between national borders, it also moves between socioeconomic classes in both directions. Was the quadrille actually a French dance, for instance, or was it just a French version of the eight-hand reel, which the rural Irish knew as a hey back in the 1500s? Did the courtiers of Europe steal it from the peasantry or vice versa?

In the end, when the Irish Dancing Commission under the auspices of the Gaelic League published its book, *Ar Rince Foirne,* of the thirty most popular ceili dances in 1929, the quadrilles had been removed in favor of Irish set dances such as the eight-hand reel and the *High Caul Cap.* By the 1920s, the Gaelic League had also opened the first of many schools to standardize the teaching of Irish step dance, taking over where the dance masters of the eighteenth and nineteenth centuries had left off.

3

Irish Dance in the Twentieth Century

Until the early 1900s, Irish dance continued to take place in towns and rural areas quite organically. House dances were an integral part of rural life. These included barn dances and "joined dances," in which many poor families pitched in money for food and drink in order to throw a dancing party. The dances were lively and raucous; at some point in the evening when a particularly talented dancer took the floor, the crowd would shout, "Take down the door!" Then the front door would be taken from its hinges and laid flat on the clay floor of the house so that the crowd might better enjoy the rhythmic sounds of the step dance.

Another kind of house dance that was common from the 1850s on was a more solemn affair called an American or Australian wake. These were goodbye parties that served as send-offs for young people who were moving to a new country in search of work and a better future.

Dances were also held outdoors on portable platforms, often

The Irish custom of informal house dances came under attack by the Catholic Church and Irish government in the early 1900s, culminating with the Public Halls Dance Act in 1936, which made it illegal to hold dances without first obtaining a permit.

at crossroads, which not only made for a common meeting place known to all, but also held a mythical allure since the earliest times as a powerful space where the forces of good and evil collided. One popular outdoors dance called a "Biddy Ball" took place on St. Brigid's Eve (January 31). Parades of villagers carried a doll known as Brideog through the countryside, stopping at each house to dance and sing for money. Later, when enough money had been collected, the crowd would buy beer and dance the night away at a "porter's ball."

All this rowdiness, drinking, and pagan undertone gave great concern to that old enemy of Irish dance, the Catholic Church.

THE PUBLIC HALLS DANCE ACT

For hundreds of years, the Catholic clergy had been fighting a losing battle to get the Irish people to stop dancing. They preached from the pulpit on the evils of men and women cavorting into the wee hours of the morning. Clergymen went so far as to hunt down crossroads dances and set the platforms on fire. Public penances were given for defying the church's orders not to dance. Most importantly, if a parishioner was found dancing, his local priest would often refuse to give him a reference, which was vitally important in getting a job, especially if he moved to another locale.

With the organizing influence of the Gaelic League's indoor, controlled ceili dances and the formation of its Irish Dancing Commission in 1930, the church saw a chance to rein in the informal, rowdy dances that troubled them so much. The bishops issued a statement on the evils of dancing, which was read at Masses in the late 1920s. Then the clergy joined up with the government and police—who were no fans of informal late-night dance parties involving alcohol either—and in 1936 the Irish government passed the Public Halls Dance Act, which made it illegal to hold a dance without first obtaining a permit. Because nearly all house and crossroads dances were held by poor rural people, the act in effect killed the tradition of these dances, which were regularly raided by the police.

The church then funded the construction of large parochial halls built just for dancing, and from then on Irish dances took place outside the home, indoors, under the watchful eye of the clergy and police.

At the same time the government was cracking down on where and when dances could be held, the Irish Dancing Commission set about standardizing the particular steps and styles that comprised Irish dance. In addition to their handbook of thirty ceili dances for groups, the commission opened step dance schools in the 1920s, which led to the publication of three books (1939, 1943, and 1969) on step dance. These three books remain the accepted standards for Irish step dance. The commission also began to train and accredit teachers, establish competitions, and employ judges to preside over them. Irish dance teachers and judges had to pass an exam to be licensed by the commission.

In order to understand how the commission's standards changed the Irish dance scene, we must first look at the regional styles of step dance that prevailed at the time. In the northern region of Ulster, step dance involved a constant drumming action made by alternately pounding the heel and toe of the supporting foot against the floor; this type of dance is hard and loud and resembles English clog dancing. The style in the western region of Connemara is more flat-footed but also employs rapid pounding of the heel and ball of the foot, similar to flamenco, and the arms are occasionally raised to shoulder height instead of being confined to the sides. The southern region of Munster's style differs from these two in that the heel is usually raised a few inches off the floor and the feet, which are slightly turned out, aren't ever allowed to go flat.

Perhaps because of the foreign influences associated with clog and flamenco dancing, and the refined image it was trying to create of Irish culture, it was the southern, Munster style that the Irish Dancing Commission codified as the standard for step dance. Thus the commission did a great service to step dance by standardizing it and establishing schools for it worldwide, but at the expense of the loss of other regional styles and the great variety of improvisation and individual expression that was historically found at house and crossroads dances.

COMPETITIVE IRISH DANCE

Irish dancing has always harbored a competitive spirit. One Gaelic phrase for dancing, *babhta rince*, translates to "a bout of dance," as if there were sure to be a winner and a loser. The dance masters of the 1800s helped foster this attitude, often challenging each other to friendly contests at county fairs. An old tradition called "dancing on the heights" further illustrates this competitive spirit: When two rival step dancers faced off, the board they danced on would be placed higher and higher for each round of dances in a sort of step-dance game of chicken; first on a barrel, then on a barrel on a table, and so on, until, by one account, two men were actually footing it on a board balanced on a chimney.[5]

With the publication of the Irish Dancing Commission's book and its licensed schools, teachers, and judges, competitive dance reached new levels. Published standards exist not only for solo step dances but also for group sets and even ceili dances, the only dance in which the hands can be raised. As its style has evolved from dancers of all ages moving up and down in a confined space with a low ceiling, to young dancers learning in the large space of a classroom, step dance has become more airborne and athletic. Now dancers travel across the stage and perform high kicks in between the cuts, grinds, and batters. Most competitors are under age eighteen, and more young women are performing step dance than ever before.

In 1969, even more competitions called *feis* (fesh), and registered schools were founded with the formation of a second dancing commission, the Organization for Irish Dance. Today in the United States alone, more than 160 competitions are held each year involving more than two thousand dancers. And this is just a small percentage of the fifty thousand Americans enrolled in Irish dance classes and the many more worldwide.

The dancing commissions preside over music and costume requirements as well as the steps. Girls wear knee-length dresses embroidered with Celtic logos, white socks, and either laced-up soft black leather shoes or hard-soled shoes with a special ankle strap for heavier dances. Their hair is traditionally long and curled into tight ringlets so that their airborne steps can be appreciated as the curls fly up on each jump. Boys wear knee socks, kilts, jackets, and ties, often with a Celtic shawl across their shoulder, and usually hard-soled shoes. Music is played by traditional ensembles called ceili bands; its melody, once provided by fiddles and uilleann pipes, is mostly performed on an accordion with accompanying fiddle, percussion, and bass.

RIVERDANCE

Most of the world, however, never got a glimpse of young girls and boys in white knee socks and kilts performing step dances

First with *Riverdance* and later *Lord of the Dance*, American-born Michael Flatley almost single-handedly made Irish dance a global phenomenon in the 1990s.

at their competitions. Irish dance remained a world unto itself: a beloved hobby for its fans and the Irish diasporas worldwide, and a possible career path for only a relatively few accredited teachers, until 1994. During that year's Eurovision Song Contest in Dublin, an interval act of Irish dancers appeared onstage. Backed by a chorus of dancers stepping in perfect time to the music of Bill Whelan, and fronted by two unbelievably talented Irish-American dancers, Michael Flatley and Jean Butler, *Riverdance* took step dancing to new levels of popularity and accessibility with its fiery Celtic hybrid music, its short costumes, and especially the high-flying athleticism of its two stars. Enrollment at Irish dance schools doubled and for the first time ever, traditional Irish dance became a viable career option for its most talented practitioners.

Riverdance proved so popular that it now has two separate touring troupes named for Irish rivers: Liffey and Lagan. When Michael Flatley left the troupe to form his own show, *Lord of the Dance*, it too rode a wave of popularity that is still ongoing. Other troupes such as *Feet of Flames*, *Spirit of Dance*, and *Gaelforce Dance* have popularized Irish dance even more— although, to be accurate, these shows are a highly theatrical and modernized brand of Irish step dance, mingled with jazz and Broadway-style moves, and bolstered by an eclectic blend of music, scenery, and dramatic plots.

With all of this professionalism and commercial success, along with the stringent standards of the Irish Dance Commission, and the Organization for Irish Dance, what had started out as pagan ritual and communal expression has evolved into something quite specialized—and spectacular.

But the Irish people weren't about to let codified steps be the only means of expression and professional dancers the only practitioners of a beloved custom they'd held for centuries.

SEAN-NOS, THE OLD STYLE

In the 1970s, while the young Michael Flatley was learning the jig at an Irish dancing school in Chicago and the National Folk Theatre was founded in Dublin, another phenomenon was being reborn in the pubs of Connemara on the west coast of Ireland.

Local patrons of all ages, whose parents and grandparents had grown up dancing the earthy, flat-footed Connemara style of step dance, full of improvisation and individual creativity, were getting up to dance solo jigs and reels as well as sets and half-sets.

With no particular costume or footwear, no rules for carrying one's arms, which would occasionally rise to shoulder level while the body swayed to the leaning of the feet, and with lots of heel-toe stamping to fast music, the residents of Connemara were reviving *sean-nos*, or old-style, step dance. One style in particular, called *timeail*, employed heavy use of clicking sounds reminiscent of Spanish dances such as flamenco. Today, with most Irish people living in towns and cities instead of on farms, sean-nos is a vital remnant of organic Irish dance, performed by regular Irish people for pure enjoyment. Sean-nos competitions still exist, but compared to other feis, they are very informal and for the most part local.

The pubs also spawned another revival for Irish set dances in the 1970s. Older people who couldn't necessarily perform skilled solos still wanted to do more than passively watch others dance—or attend structured ceilithe—so they began to take classes in set dances such as the Caledonian and the Connemara. Nowadays, set dancers travel throughout the country studying the various regional differences, intent on preserving all traditional nuances of these group dances. What they learn they then take to the pub on a Saturday night and perform with their neighbors. It seems the inborn Irish need to dance will never be totally confined to classroom, ballroom, or stage, but will happen naturally and spontaneously wherever the Gaelic spirit moves a group of people to get up and step a jig.

4

The Roots of Polish Dancing

Poland, a country about the size of the state of New Mexico, sits at the geographical center of Europe on the northern coast of the continent, south of the Baltic Sea. It is surrounded by Germany on the west, the Czech Republic and Slovakia to the south, and Belarus and Ukraine to the east.

Since its inception in the tenth century, Poland has had an exceedingly tumultuous history, progressing over the next thousand years from a feudal kingdom to one of Europe's greatest powers before disappearing entirely from the map as it was partioned by three of its neighbors. It reclaimed its sovereignty after World War I only to come under Soviet control after World War II and finally, in 1989, reemerged as an independent, democratic republic.

During all this time, the Polish people continued to nurture their folk dance customs as well as other aspects of their culture with a fierce sense of identity, developing not

Despite a history filled with upheaval, Poland was able to maintain its cultural identity and is well-known for its varied folk dance.

only five national dances, but also hundreds of regional dances that are still performed in rural areas and by folk dance troupes onstage.

THE PAGAN SLAVS

The Polish people descend from the large tribe called the Slavs, who migrated from their homeland in Asia to what is now eastern Europe sometime between 3000 and 2000 B.C. and then, beginning around 400 A.D., began to fan out westward and southward, eventually settling the countries we now know as the Czech Republic, Slovakia, Belarus, Ukraine, Russia, Serbia, Croatia, Slovenia, Bosnia, and Montenegro. The Polish, along with their neighbors, the Czechs and Slovaks, are from the western branch of the Slavs.

The name Poland comes from the Slavic word "pole," or field, so named because much of the country consists of low-lying fields and forests, the only highlands being the Carpathian Mountains in the south.

The early Slavs organized themselves into familial clans and cultivated crops such as peas, turnips, flax, and rye. Later they also raised sheep, cows, pigs, and goats. The Slavs had no official priesthood or government. Led typically by the elderly people of their clan, they worshipped pagan gods of nature, and like the Celts, these gods were often associated with trees. They considered the oak to be particularly powerful as it was the sacred tree of the thunder god Perun.

The Slavs found many reasons to dance. Most of these dances were part of magical rituals to cure the sick, win battles, bless newlyweds, and honor the dead. The majority of the dances centered on the harvest and the change of seasons. Their earliest dances were probably simple circle formations in which they sang, clapped, and stamped their feet around a tree, a fire, or a symbolic object.

For instance, as in Ireland, the Slavs danced round bonfires and maypoles on May Day. And at the end of the harvest, women would take the last stalks of the rye crop and dance around them to ensure a good crop the following year, when they would mix the old stalks, which had been thus blessed, into the new seed. In the custom of the "rye mother," a powerful spirit believed to have been left standing in the field after the harvest, an older married woman would shape the last stalks into a straw-woman, dress the figure in women's clothes, and let it be carried through the village where it would become the center of a harvest supper and dance.

THE POLISH KINGDOM AND THE CHURCH

After the Slavic migration of the fifth century, class distinctions, and eventually feudalism, began to take root, as princes and territories emerged from Slavic subtribes such as the Polanie and Wislanie. The first Polish kingdom was formed in 966 A.D. when the Polanie Duke Mieszko married the Czech Princess Dabrowka, under whose terms he agreed to be baptized into the Roman Catholic Church. From this point on, the Polish Slavs began their conversion to Christianity.

In the prior century, the Holy Roman Emperor, Charlemagne, whose empire covered all of western Europe right up to Poland's borders, prohibited all forms of dancing. We can assume the Catholic Church had similar orders for Poland, as both Mieszko and his heir, Boleslaw I, relied heavily on the protection of the Pope, whose was not only a religious leader but also had political, military, and economic power as well. Dioceses, then called bishoprics, began springing up all over Poland as Boleslaw set out to use the church's power and in the process convert the Slavs from their pagan ways.

But, as happened in Ireland, while the proposed meaning of many rituals changed to Christian themes, the original melodies and dances remained.

For example, all across Europe pre-Christians participated in the spring custom of "burying death," a ritual that celebrated the end of winter's darkness and the resurrection of spring by banning or destroying a symbolic figure of death. In Poland, that figure could be a straw man paraded through the village before being burned in effigy or a straw woman carried to the village boundary toward the setting sun, then torn apart; its pieces scattered among the fields or thrown into water. When the church prohibited dancing during Lent, the *flaxwise dance*, in which married women jumped as high as they wanted the crops to grow, became an Ash Wednesday tradition, marking the beginning of Lent.

Village religious processions eventually formed the basis of the Polish *chodzony*, a simple walking dance that is often practiced at church ceremonies, christenings, weddings, and funerals.

In each case, what was once a pagan celebration gradually became a pre-Lenten rite; the pretext changed, but the ritual itself didn't.

Many of these rituals also involved processions of marchers walking through the village. This simple processional at a walking pace—also practiced at church ceremonies as well as christenings, weddings, and funerals—became known as the *chodzony* (hoh-dzoh-nih), from the word *chodzic*, to walk. It usually involved a parade of couples of all ages walking hand in hand or linked by holding each end of a handkerchief or hat. They were accompanied at first by their own singing, later by slow, simple music played on violins, tambourines or drums, and bagpipes.

The chodzony was often begun inside a house by the highest-ranking couple, usually the oldest or most important man and his wife. The man would start by singing a song and then leading the party in a circle, or a winding serpentine pattern, or a "bridge" in which one column of couples passed under the raised arms of another column. The front man could lead the procession over chairs, tables, and even through windows, eventually taking them outside. Throughout the dance, the lead male could be replaced as another man came forward to start his own song, thus "cutting in" and taking the lead female's hand. The chodzony was especially popular at weddings, when every man wanted a chance to take the lead and dance with the bride.

In yet another example of how traditional dance evolves between social classes, the chodzony, a simple peasant dance, formed the basis of the polonez, which would later turn up in Poland's royal court at the marriage of a king.

KRAKOW AND THE KRAKOWIAK

The centuries following the Polish kingdom's birth saw many threats to its existence, both from warring nobles within and from invasions by the Mongols in the thirteenth century and the Teutonic Knights in the fifteenth century. However, Poland continued not only to survive but thrive. Advances in agriculture along with the mining of gold, silver, and coal added to the nation's wealth. The Roman Catholic Church brought art and architecture to the nation as first Romanesque and then Gothic cathedrals and palaces were built.

The kingdom reached its apogee with the 1384 marriage of Queen Jadwiga to Jagiello of Lithuania. The marriage united the two countries, beginning a reign of 400 years in which Poland grew to be one of Europe's largest powers.

The city of Krakow played a central role in Poland's rise. It held Wawel Castle, where the king and his court resided. It was the home of Poland's first university, founded in 1364. In the late 1490s, the University of Krakow produced Nicolaus Copernicus, who revolutionized astronomy with his discovery that the Earth revolved around the sun, and not vice versa. After the invention of the printing press in the fifteenth century, Krakow became an important European printing center.

The villages around Krakow were the breeding ground for one of Poland's five national dances, the *krakowiak*, named for the nearby city. A quick, exuberant dance, the krakowiak began to be seen in the fourteenth century at weddings, baptisms, or simply on Sundays when villagers rested from working. A local tavern was often the setting for these events.

Some theorize that the krakowiak may have been inspired by the movements of the horse, an animal much-admired by the Polish, because its basic traveling step is a smooth *chassé* in which the leading foot slides out and then the other foot follows, snapping the feet together in a slight hop. When repeated, this movement resembles a horse's gallop.

The krakowiak was danced by several couples, each man and woman facing their partner and holding on by the waist or shoulders. As with the chodzony, the dance began with a man starting a familiar or improvised song before the musicians, then proceeding to lead the couples in a gallop around the room; often the leader would intersperse the gallops with stamps, turns, and heel clicks, which the others would imitate. The dancers moved in formations of circles, serpentines, or diagonals, sometimes breaking into an inner circle of linked women facing an outer circle of linked men.

From the villages around Krakow, the dance spread to the nobility, who made their own additions and embellishments to the basic galloping step. From there, the dance's lively, joyous air made it infectious, and it spread throughout the entire country, back to each region and among all the classes.

Several centuries later, the krakowiak was made famous by the Viennese ballerina Fanny Elssler when she performed it under the name *cracovienne* on her tours of Europe and America in 1839. The krakowiak can be heard in Frederic Chopin's "Rondo a la Krakowiak," Op. 14. It remains popular in Poland today and is often the first dance children learn. With more than fifty individual steps and numerous floor patterns, its varieties are nearly endless.

THE POLONEZ

If the krakowiak is an example of how a folk dance can spread throughout a country, the *polonez* shows how it can spread beyond the country's borders throughout an entire continent.

Remember the humble chodzony, the peasant dance popular at weddings? In the fifteenth and sixteenth centuries, this processional dance made its way first to the petty gentry in the country, then to the nobility, and finally to the royal court. In the process, the music became livelier and the processional more and more fanciful and aristocratic, with each man holding his arm straight out in front of him while his partner placed her hand genteelly over his.

It was danced as a formal march in 1573 when the Frenchman Henry Valois was elected king of Poland. From then on it became a staple of court dance, often opening royal balls so that elaborately dressed aristocrats got a chance to display their finery—the men often in full military regalia, the women in long flowing gowns—and make introductory small talk during their slow, stately walk. In the towns, the dress would be much plainer, but by the late 1600s, it was danced by all the social strata in Poland.

The dance made its way to Germany, Russia, and France in the 1700s, where it became known as the *polonaise*. In the 1800s, composers such as Frederic Chopin, Beethoven, and Handel began composing polonez music. Chopin's "Polonaise Militaire,"

THE POLONEZ

In the basic stance of the *polonez*, each couple stands side by side, facing forward. The man stands to the left of the woman, extending his right hand out in front of him, while she places her left hand gently on his. From this fundamental position, the couple walks with other couples in figures such as one or more circles, long diagonal lines, or a "bridge" running down the middle of the room under which other couples pass. Performed in triple-time, like a very slow waltz, the basic step of the polonez consists of a somewhat long, regal walk in which the knees bend slightly on every first step, punctuating the waltz-like quality of the dance. The torso is held erect and the chin high; even facial gestures are important in this dance, as one may never appear strained or overzealous, but calm and graceful, and should glance frequently at one's partner. In addition to the basic walking step, the man may pass the woman to his left and then back again, leading her by the arm. In another common step, the couple stop to face each other, linked hands held high between them, and take a step toward each other and then back. Several times during a polonez, as the music slows into what is called a *ritardando*, the partners face each other to bow, the man lowering his head and the woman executing a curtsy while holding out her long dress. After the bow, the dance then proceeds onto the next figure. The dance ends with a long bow.

The *polonez*, one of Poland's five national dances, spread to all of Europe in the 1700s and even influenced classical ballet.

Op. 40, No. 2, for instance, is one famous example of the dance's slow tempo punctuated by a drawn-out ending note during which the dancers bow. The polonez can also be seen in the George Balanchine ballets *Theme and Variations* and in the "Diamonds" segment of *Jewels*.

The polonez survives as one of Poland's five national dances to this day, and its dignified steps make it known as the "grand march of Poland."

5

From the Fields to the Palaces and Back

The sixteenth century was known as Poland's Golden Age. Its union with Lithuania made it one of Europe's largest countries, with a population of eight million, of whom 67 percent were rural peasants, 23 percent were townspeople, and 10 percent were nobles and clergy. Relative to other European countries, Poland had a very high percentage of nobles, many of who owned several villages.

Because of their wealth and mobility, the Polish gentry both exported and imported Polish culture as they traveled and traded throughout the continent. Their strong numbers also empowered them to push for more governmental rights, and by the late sixteenth century, the Polish monarchy became an elected one with two parliamentary houses, the Senate and House of Deputies.

Polish peasants, or serfs, though they owned no land, also prospered during this time. Thanks to grain and timber exports,

In the *zbojnicki*, Polish highlanders from the Tatra Mountains in southern Poland carry hatchets, sing, and leap high off the ground.

the Polish economy was booming and the peasant population growing. Culturally, the Italian Renaissance was reaching Poland's borders and religious orders were building schools, gymnasiums, and colleges. Though these institutions, built for the gentry, didn't directly affect the peasants, the rich cultural and social fabric of Poland's great cities was a source of pride for the general population and an attractive vision to Poland's neighbors as well. By 1540, composer Jan Lublin's songbook *Organ Tablature* contained twenty-seven Polish dances.

REGIONAL DANCES

One example of how diverse and rich the cultural fabric of the Polish countryside was can be seen in the fact that each of the nation's five major regions had its own wealth of traditional dances. Because the Polish landscape was thickly forested and strewn with rivers and swamps, these five geographic regions each gave birth to their own styles of folk dance:

- In **Pomerania**, the northwestern area of Poland that borders the Baltic Sea, dances usually have two parts and use singing, clapping, gesturing, and props.

- In **Silesia**, the southwestern area bordering the Czech Republic, dances use fast tempos and syncopated rhythms.

- **Malopolska** is also called Little Poland, and it is the only mountainous region of the country, containing the Tatra range in the Carpathian Mountains. Many ethnic groups such as the Tatra highlanders reside there, and dances tend to focus on the men's stomps and jumps; in one, a single man dances with every woman, each woman introducing him to the next. One example of a highlander dance is the *zbojnicki* or hatchet dance.

- **Wielkopolska**, or Greater Poland, is the central western area of the country. Dances here often feature one couple leading a group of other couples.

- **Mazovia** and **Mazuria** are the eastern regions of the country. Their dances show influences from Russia and Ukraine, which they border, and a common pattern is a group of couples whirling around in a circle.

Within these five regions, Poland has forty distinct folkloric regions. The diversity of dance customs was nearly endless. The accompanying music was usually in triple meter—like the 1-2-3 of the waltz—although there were exceptions. Dances were highly improvisational, and usually began when a man approached the gathered musicians, paid them, and they followed his lead as he sang a song, often improvising on the spot. This man became the lead dancer and the group would follow his movements. Male dancers played a significant role, and although most dances called for couples, the men of the group got the most attention, displayed the most creativity and diversity of movement, and, as in Ireland, often made the tone of the dance a competitive one.

In addition to great diversity within its borders, Poland's central location in Europe meant it was surrounded by numerous, and often dangerous, neighbors. Beginning in 1665, Poland had to fight the Ukranian Cossacks, the Swedes, and the Turks. The central government was also weakened by individual veto powers granted to Parliament, whose members used their votes as political weapons against one another.

By the 1700s, when the ideals of the European Enlightenment—knowledge, freedom, reason—were spreading throughout the continent, the Polish townspeople began to push for a more democratic and centralized government. While the ruling gentry rested on its laurels, the middle classes began to build schools, print newspapers, and express nationalist sentiments. But all this proved too late: In the late eighteenth century, three of Poland's neighbors—Russia, Prussia (today northeastern Germany), and Austria—took advantage of its weakened condition and invaded. By 1795, what used to be Poland was parceled as Galicia (owned by Austria), the Polish Kingdom (under the rule of Russia), and the Grand Duchy of Warsaw (ruled by Prussia). Poland no longer existed as a nation and would remain under foreign rule for the next 123 years.

THE MAZUR

The annexation of Poland as a country would seemingly devastate its cultural practices. But just the opposite happened. As the partitioners sought to destroy anything "Polish," Polish culture, especially its folk dance,

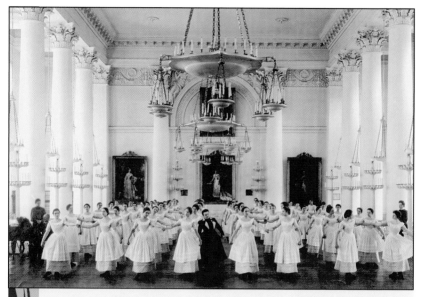

The *Mazur*, or *Mazurka* in English, is named for the Mazury, a Slavic tribe of east-central Poland, who started the dance in the 1500s. The couples dance eventually spread first to the Polish aristocracy then throughout Europe in the 1700s.

continued to thrive not only inside the borders of the former country but throughout Europe as well.

Two examples, as we have seen, were the polonez and the krakowiak, which spread to western European ballrooms and to the ballet stage in the 1800s even though Poland, per se, did not exist during that century. Another Polish peasant dance that reached the peak of its popularity at this time was the *mazur*.

The mazur was danced all the way back to the 1500s by the Mazury, one of the Slavic tribes in east-central Poland, from whom it derives its name. A lively circle dance for couples often accompanied by bagpipes, the mazur is distinctive for its turns, during which the couple links either hands or elbows, more similar to the turns seen in square dancing.

These basics don't even begin to describe the mazur, however, as improvisation (by men) forms a good part of the dance and there are more than fifty mazur steps and one hundred floor patterns.

By the seventeenth century, the mazur had spread from the peasants of Mazuria to the royal courts in Krakow, where it became more stylized and sophisticated. From there, the aristocracy took it back with them to townspeople throughout the country and also to Russia, London, Paris, Spain, Scandinavia, and Hungary, where it became known as the *mazurka*. During the American presidency of James Madison in the early 1800s, his wife Dolly introduced it at a ball at the White House. Later in the 1800s the mazurka was incorporated into such famous ballets as *Swan Lake*, *The Sleeping Beauty*, and *Coppelia*, and again, composer Frederic Chopin wrote several mazurkas.

The mazur's most memorable contribution to Polish identity, however, had to do with its popularity among the Polish Legions, young soldiers of the aristocracy who joined Napoleon's forces in 1797 in an effort to bolster their own fight to regain Poland's independence from Austria. The officers' training included proper dancing of the mazur, and they danced it at all their ceremonies in full military uniform. Dancing the mazur, and singing the songs that accompanied it, became a symbol of Polish pride and nationalism.

When the legion was stationed in Italy with Napoleon's troops in 1797, they needed a marching song. So one of the soldiers, Jozef Wybicki, who was also a poet, composed inspiring words to an old folk mazur tune and sang them to the troops, beginning with the words, "Poland is not dead as long as we live." The song, which became known as "Dabrowski's mazurka," caught on and continued to be sung by the Polish people throughout their 123-year struggle for independence until, in 1926, it finally became Poland's national anthem. The mazur is now one of Poland's five national dances.

THE KUJAWIAK

Another dance that surged in popularity during this time, though similar to the mazur in musical structure, was more concerned with romance than with patriotism. The *kujawiak*, another of Poland's national dances, began in the villages of the agricultural Kujawy region in central Poland. It featured couples spinning slowly as they also moved in a circle.

It was often performed in conjunction with the two other dances; the simple walking dance or chodzony would precede it, and the livelier turning mazur would follow. The romantic, lyrical kujawiak would be the centerpiece of the dance. Eventually these three merged into one, and now the kujawiak may begin with a processional, diverge into its distinctive slow turns, and end with faster movements similar to the mazur.

Kujawiak songs, often written in a minor chord, have a lilting, melancholy quality about them. Any lyrics are usually what we'd consider a "love song." The music was traditionally played on violin in concert with a bass, drum, clarinet, and bagpipes.

Unlike the mazur, the kujawiak, in keeping with its romantic feeling, is danced with the couple facing each other, hands linked either in the classic "ballroom" position or with the woman's hands on the man's shoulders and his hands on her waist. Sometimes both partners put their hands on each other's shoulders. It incorporates deep knee bends and graceful leaning from side to side.

The kujawiak proved so popular among the peasantry that the landowners became curious. They invited village dancers and musicians to their estates in order to learn the steps and figures. Of course, the dance quickly spread to the balls of the nobility, where its dignified gracefulness made a lasting impression—and it was then returned to the towns in changed form.

FOLK DANCE'S EVOLUTION

As you can see in the descriptions of Poland's national dances, a predictable pattern emerged for each one. The dance originated in rural areas among members of an ethnic group, then was adopted by the nobility, who sometimes embellished it with their own steps. From there, the modified dance was embraced by the townspeople all the way "down" to the rural peasants again, who continued to make their own changes as well. These progressions were natural and inevitable and have been studied by scholars. As the dance progressed from an organic, often ritualistic practice, to a popular form enjoyed by society en masse, scholars note several distinctions:

- The most organic, oldest form is called ethnic dance, which simply means that it is practiced by a certain ethnic group, tribe, or region. Ethnic dances are ritualistic, meaning the steps evolve out of a natural urge to commune with nature or the supernatural; to observe rites of passage such as marriage or birth; or to prepare for important events such as war or the harvest. Ethnic dance is commonly called folk dance, although it's important to understand that "folk dance" is a recent phrase. While it can refer to an ethnic dance, more often these days it refers to a preserved or modified ethnic dance, which is no longer danced in its original context.

- Once an ethnic/folk dance is adopted by the population en masse, it often takes the characteristics of social dance. This is where the categories can merge, for many social dances are still considered folk dances and vice versa. The main distinction is that folk/ethnic dances originate from a specific cultural context such as a harvest, a wedding, or a religious rite. Once the dance becomes a social dance, it can be danced anywhere, anytime; removed from its original context. Its pretext becomes the sheer enjoyment of dancing.

The *mazur* is often adapted from its folk routes into theatrical performances such as the *Cinderella Ballet*. Here, Osmay Molina, and the Nacional Ballet de Cuba perform the *mazur*.

- The next step in the migration involves the move from social to *theatrical dance,* when the dance actually ceases to be participatory and instead is danced onstage with added dramatic elements. Here again, the distinctions merge, because even an ethnic dance can be "watched" by some members who might be considered an "audience," but by and large its basic context is participatory, while the basic context of theatrical dance involves a passive audience and active performers on a stage. An obvious example is when folk dances such as the mazur are incorporated into ballets, thus becoming theatrical versions of themselves. But another, more complex example is when professional folk dance ensembles put on regional costumes and dance ethnic/folk dances onstage for an audience.

THE ZBOJNICKI

This *zbojnicki* (zbooy-neets-kee), or hatchet dance, comes from the Tatra Mountains in southern Poland. It is performed by men only, dressed in traditional long pants, wide belts, white shirts, moccasins, and flat round hats and holding an old type of mountain hatchet. The hatchet is long, with a pointed metal spike at the bottom and a steel ax at top—and it's real, so the dancers must be careful! In olden days, the hatchet was used for mountain climbing or to fight off wild animals; now it is used as a walking stick or for ornamentation in dances like this one.

The men begin by singing while standing in a straight line, their hatchets held up in the right hand, facing the musicians who sit off to the side playing fiddles, violins, and bass. As they sing, they might shake the hatchets or hit them together to the beat. They then fall into a circle, walking with a natural gait, until the leader calls out a command at which they face toward the center of the circle and begin a series of acrobatic squats all the way to the ground, kicking up first one leg, then the other as they come out of each squat, often ending the series of squats with a high leap in which both knees bend as the heels fly up behind. The men continue alternating their walking and singing with their acrobatic interludes—which may also include passing the hatchets under their knees or tossing them between each other. The dance ends the way it began, the men in a straight line, finishing their song while hitting the hatchets together.

6

Poland and Its Culture Survive

Throughout the 1800s, the partitioned Polish territory fought to regain its independence with guns, with social changes that finally enfranchised the peasants, with newspapers, and with an entire, organized underground government. Under great strain, the Polish people fought desperately to maintain their cultural identity. Romanticism, the philosophical and artistic movement that exalted human emotion and sentiment over science and dispassion, was flourishing in Europe at the time, and Polish writers and musicians excelled in producing works that lauded the underdog, the idealistic man, and the struggle for freedom. At the same time, an ideology called Positivism captured the Polish imagination. It promoted an organized, self-disciplined, hardworking approach to work, education, and economics. Poland was determined not to let its rich and deeply beloved cultural heritage die.

The *polka*, a simple waltz-like dance, actually has its origins in early nineteenth-century Bohemia, a region of the Czech Republic, and not Poland. The dance quickly spread throughout Europe and by mid-century was the most popular dance on the continent.

THE POLKA

Poland's seat at the crossroads of Europe meant that for several centuries it had served as a gateway between the northern Scandinavians and the southern Slavs, as well as between the western Europeans and the Russians to the east. This central geographical and economic position, along with its many clashes and encounters with its neighbors, made Poland's borders extremely permeable to foreign influence. In dance, these influences showed up in such forms as the waltz from Austria and the czardas from Hungary.

But its biggest dance import by far was the *polka*, the dance that is most closely associated with Poland but that actually originated in Bohemia, a province of the Czech Republic, in the early nineteenth century. According to legend, the polka, which means "Polish-like" or "Polish maiden," was first danced by a Bohemian girl named Anna Slezak upon hearing news that her lover, a soldier, was alive. Scholars note the oddity of a dance started by a Bohemian girl being named "Polish maiden" and also theorize that the name polka may have come from the Czech word *pulka* or "half," correlating to the basic step that repeats first on one leg, then another, evenly splitting the motion in half.

Wherever it originated and however it was named, by 1840, the polka had spread through all of Europe. At first the basic polka step—hop, step, step, step—was danced in various formations by couples, with the spinning motion often the last formation. But all the figures soon gave way to the constant spinning step we know today.

In the mid-nineteenth century, the polka became the most popular dance in Europe. Polkas appeared in the ballrooms of London, Paris, Vienna, and all across the continent. Women's hemlines were raised to show off their polka footwork and fashions, such as "polka dots," were even named for the dance. Its steps were also introduced into the stately quadrille figures. Today, the two-step and the foxtrot are descendants of the polka. While it is still danced in ballrooms, by professional folk ensembles and in some rural areas as well, its primary form exists in the United States as the Polish-American polka.

THE OBEREK

Of the five national Polish folk dances, the last one to gain wide popularity was the *oberek*, a fast dance that, like its cousin the mazur, originated in the region of Mazovia. Sometimes also called the *oberta*, oberek comes from the Polish verb "to spin," and that is in essence what the couple dancing the oberek does; they spin faster and faster as the music progresses.

Because the oberek migrated out of its original region into mass consciousness much later than many other dances, it has retained more of its basic qualities and is still danced much as Mazovian peasants had danced it centuries ago—though today it is also performed by accomplished folk dance troupes, who lend an acrobatic and improvisational twist to the basic spinning step. The dance usually begins with a group of couples running a circle around the dancing space, as if to outline it. After that, each couple is free to improvise, in between spins, various kinds of stomps and footwork. The man in particular has an acrobatic range of steps to choose from, leaping high in the air or squatting all the way to the ground while holding his partner. Men also lift women into the air during the oberek. Often, other couples will pause to notice and admire a particular virtuosic male dancer, and an element of competition can then enter the dance with the men trying to outdo one another.

By the end of the nineteenth century, all of Poland was dancing the oberek—except, of course, that, officially and politically, the country of Poland hadn't truly existed for 105 years.

NEW CENTURY, NEW HOPE

The twentieth century finally brought a turnaround for the Polish people in the ironic form of the first World War, which pitted two of Poland's partitioners—Germany (which by this time included the former Prussia) and Austria—against the third, Russia. When Russia emerged on the winning side after WWI, Germany and Austria lost their territorial rights to Poland, but Russia also had to forsake its claim when the 1917 Bolshevik Revolution overthrew the Russian czar. Thus in 1918, Poland became a free country for the first time in 123 years. The Poles had to rebuild their political and economic systems from the ground up amid high inflation and rampant unemployment, and with three-fourths of the people still residing in the countryside.

Their sovereignty lasted only twenty years before they were again torn in two by Germany and Russia, both of which occupied Poland for six years during World War II. Poland lost 6.5 million people, more percentage-wise of its population than any other

European nation, many of them to concentration camps and Soviet labor camps. Yet their government, press, and educational system once again went underground and continued to survive. But when the war ended this time, the powers that negotiated the peace treaties put Poland under Soviet control, and it remained so for the next half century, until 1989.

Throughout these upheavals, however, Polish culture once again continued its incredible ability to thrive against all odds. Even under Soviet rule, the Poles continued to seek out educational and social reforms, often led by a thriving locus of underground intellectuals. As early as 1930, Polish scholars began to collect, document and study the nation's many dances at the University of Warsaw's Department of Ethnology. In 1948, the country's first state dance troupe, Mazowsze, was created, and 1953 saw the founding of its second: the Slask Song and Dance Ensemble. From 1968–81, the Institute of Art at the Polish Academy of Sciences in Warsaw documented the dances of various regions.

In addition to their culture, the Poles also took great comfort in their Catholic faith. The 1978 ordination of Polish Cardinal Karol Wojtyla as Pope John Paul II, and the 1980 Nobel Peace Prize for Literature being awarded to Polish writer Czeslaw Milosz helped bolster the Polish spirit. The decade that followed saw the formation of Solidarity, an extremely popular trade union that also worked for political freedom from Soviet rule and was headed by populist leader Lech Walesa. Finally, in 1989, elections were held and Poland freed itself from the Soviets and once again became the Republic of Poland.

POLISH DANCE TODAY

Today the tradition of Polish dance lives on mostly through professional and amateur folk dance ensembles whose members perform regional and national dances for enjoyment, entertainment, and competition. With elaborate costumes and live traditional music, these troupes preserve the look and feel

Polish Americans keep their folk dances alive to this day, as this group of dancers from North Dakota shows. The *Polka* is danced throughout the United States, and Polka music is recognized by the Grammy Awards, which hands out an award for Polka Album of the Year.

of the peasant dances from long ago—but not their original meaning, as we have seen in the last chapter. With urbanization, which came relatively late to Poland due to its many political struggles, few folk dances are regularly done anymore, except in some isolated rural areas. The main place to witness spontaneous Polish folk dancing today would most certainly be at a Polish wedding, when all the old dances are revived.

In addition to the many ensembles within Poland, the Polish diasporas, who immigrated to the United States, Germany, France, and Brazil in large numbers in the late nineteenth and early twentieth centuries, also gravitated to community centers, ballrooms, and church basements throughout the world to dance the mazur, the krakowiak, and the polka. The United States has such troupes in every major city.

Polish folk dance and music is lively and celebratory; it captures the unique and resilient spirit of the Polish people who built a great country, watched it fall, and then refused to

POLKAMANIA THEN AND NOW

Back in the nineteenth century, the polka was a simple dance in which the couple faced each other in the classic "ballroom" hold while performing a hop and three steps first to one side, then turning and repeating on the other. In this way the couple slowly spun round as they moved in a circle.

As the dance spread, it took on many variations: The cross-step polka, instead of incorporating a hop and three steps, used soft chassés that brushed the feet along the floor. The polka-mazurka used the triple-time of the mazurka and the basic polka steps. Perhaps the easiest rendition was the heel-and-toe polka, a slower version in which the dancers touched first the heel, then the toe of one foot to the floor before taking three steps.

Though the "heel and toe and away we go" polka is still popular in the United States today because of its simplicity, the polka that millions of Americans dance now is much different than what used to be danced in Europe. After catching on in Europe, the polka came across the Atlantic Ocean in the late nineteenth and early twentieth centuries with the waves of Polish immigrants who tired of the oppressive rule of Poland's partitioners. Forced for many years to stifle their own culture, they began forming associations, Polish-American churches, and clubs where they could gather and embrace their Polish customs in their new home. Of all the popular dances of the time, the only one that has survived en masse is the polka. In working-class neighborhoods all across the East Coast and Midwest, immigrants gathered to dance the polka and to listen to polka bands.

After World War II, Chicago became a hotbed for polka musicians like Li'l Wally, who added more expressive lyrics and give up until they had it back again. Perhaps that is what draws so many people to learn the vibrant, happy dances preserved in the Polish folk repertoire.

also clarinet and trumpet to the songs. Polka also burgeoned in the cities of Buffalo and New York and throughout Wisconsin. Rivalries between East Coast and Midwest polka even sprang up. Today there are thriving polka communities in California, New England, and many Mid-Atlantic states as well.

Eventually, the steps became livelier and more complex, with couples spinning in fanciful patterns around each other much like a fast jitterbug, yet all the while performing the basic polka step, which has now become much lighter than in the past. Watch a couple dance the polka from the waist up and you'll see lots of hopping straight up and down, but look below and you'll find their feet tracing intricate figures around the floor while continually spinning and weaving their arms around each other.

The current polka is no longer confined to only Polish Americans but is enjoyed by second- and third-generation Germans, Czechs, and eastern Europeans as well as just about anyone who wants to join in the fun. Polka dances and festivals abound; aficionados sign up for polka cruises and polka vacations. Chicago houses a Polka Music Hall of Fame and so does Cleveland, Ohio. Polka has been recognized by the Grammy Awards with a category for album of the year, and several organizations such as the International Polka Association and the United States Polka Association keep members updated on the national polka circuit.

Nearly every country has some form of polka—not only the Czech Republic, where it originated, and Poland, where it took root, but also Italy, Australia, Finland, and Mexico, among many others. But today, America is its new home.

7

The Roots of Spanish Dancing

Spain, the second largest country in Europe, occupies most of the Iberian Peninsula, a huge piece of land that juts out from the southwestern part of the continent into the Atlantic Ocean and the Mediterranean Sea and is surrounded by water on three sides. In its northeast corner, the Pyrenees Mountains separate Spain from the rest of Europe and its closest neighbor, France, while its southernmost point lies only eight miles from the northern tip of Morocco in Africa.

Spain's location at the outermost edge of Europe, its proximity to Africa, and its size (almost as large as the state of California) have all played a part in fostering a mixture of religions and peoples as well as developing an enigmatic culture all its own, somewhat isolated, intensely proud, and intriguingly unique.

A STEW OF PEOPLES AND CULTURES
Humans have inhabited the Iberian Peninsula for hundreds of

Spain's dance has been influenced by a number of civilizations, including the Celts and Moors. The Celts settled the Iberian Peninsula, which includes Spain and Portugal, in the eighth century B.C., while the Moors, who came from North Africa, invaded the peninsula in the 700s.

thousands of years, and by the eighth century B.C. the indigenous Iberians, as well as the Phoenician (present-day Lebanese) traders, who had settled on the southern coast, were joined by a branch of the Celts—the same tribe who in their northward migration ended up in Ireland. Though the Celts settled mainly in the northern and central parts of the peninsula, by 500 B.C., the people as a whole were known as the Celtic-Iberians. They were not a primitive people. Their civilization was urban-based, with city-states similar to those of Greece and Rome, and they developed their own system of writing.

They soon became known for their passionate style of dancing. The *puellae gaditanae*, Celtic-Iberian dancing girls, became famous for their seductive dances which involved difficult footwork, sensual hip movements, and shell castanets. Their dances could be ritualistic preparations for war or worship, or performed simply for pure enjoyment. After the Romans conquered Spain in the third century B.C., the dancers were regularly sent to Rome to entertain the emperor.

Rome eventually adopted Christianity, and from 589 A.D. all the way up until the twentieth century, Catholicism was Spain's official religion. It didn't have much time to take root before the Moors (African Muslims) invaded the peninsula in an effort to spread their faith northward in 711. The Iberians clung steadfastly to Christianity and struggled against Moorish occupation for the next six centuries, but Spain's music, art, and architecture were heavily influenced by the Moorish occupation, and so was its dance. The curving, sinuous arm movements, use of shawls and wide skirts, and irregular musical phrasings—moving from fast rhythms to long pauses—can all be traced to Middle-Eastern and North African roots.

Many dances of medieval Spain remained pagan in origin, and thus resembled the seasonal and magical practices of other Europeans. Young girls in Galicia, in northwestern Spain, for example, dance with swords and around poles to celebrate the coming of spring. An all-male dance in the Basque region in northeastern Spain challenges each man to leap higher than the others, harkening back to magical dances aimed at helping crops grow tall. A street dance from Catalonia in the northeastern corner of the country, called the *Ball de la Tey*, concludes with a tree being burned, reminiscent of the tree worship seen throughout pre-Christian Europe.

As the Moorish occupation drew on and the fighting between Christians and Moors stretched over the centuries, one popular dance was invented to commemorate Spain's struggles. The *morisca*, also known as *Moros y Cristianos*, portrayed a mock battle between the Moors and Christians, with participants using either real swords or sticks or scarves as stand-ins. One of the earliest moriscas was performed at a royal wedding in Lerida in 1150, and from then on it became a widespread dance performed at tournaments, banquets, and in the royal courts of feudal Spain. (Moriscas also appeared later in Italy, eastern Europe, and Turkey as the Moorish invaders spread eastward from Spain.)

DANCING WITHIN THE CHURCH

By the 1100s, Spain was beginning to gain an upper hand in its struggle against the Moors as Christian kings entered from the north, regaining territory back for the Catholic Church. For some reason, the church in Spain—perhaps understanding that the people of Spain had a love for their native dances—proved much more accepting of dance than in other countries. They allowed dance to be performed within the church, right up at the altar. One example is the *danzas* of the early Renaissance, dances with religious themes such as the Christmas story, which were performed by villagers and shepherds.

Another example that survives today in the cities of Seville and Toledo is a practice celebrating the Catholic holy days of Corpus Christi in June and the Immaculate Conception in December. *Los Seises*, or "the sixes," was so named because it was performed by twelve young choirboys in two rows of six, wearing white shoes and stockings with either blue or red robes, and holding ivory castanets. The boys, having been trained by dancing masters hired by the church, performed slow, elegant walking and gliding steps that gave the dance a lyrical but solemn tone. Los Seises was danced typically at the evening mass, in front of the altar on which stood the chalice of the Holy Sacrament, surrounded by flickering candles. The vision of children dancing, and the clergy and congregation kneeling, all in homage to a Catholic feast day is perhaps one of the few surviving examples of how dance could be made sacred within the church.

The church also teamed up with local governments to

The *sevillanas*, a dance that originated in the seventeenth century, comes from the region around Seville in southern Spain and is referred to as the "mother of Spanish dance." One of several courtship dances throughout Spain, the *sevillanas* is performed by a couple who weave around one another before pausing suddenly in between *coplas* or improvised verses.

sponsor processional dances for religious or national celebrations, hiring professional dancers, dressing them in elaborate costumes, and parading them from the cathedral along the processional route through town for everyone to enjoy.

Spanish popular dance around this time employed much hand clapping, singing, stamping, acrobatics, tumbling, and, of course, the use of castanets. Merchants' fairs held in town plazas typically concluded with dancing at night. Before long, dance masters appeared—wandering men with guitars and violins holding lessons in taverns, cafes, and plazas—teaching villagers and townspeople the popular dances of the day. Though some dance masters also taught the upper class in dance academies, these typically excluded women and the steps taught there were not as lively as the versions performed in the villages. These two styles gave rise to two distinct Spanish words for dance: *baile*, meaning the more popular style with livelier arm and torso movements, and danza, the more controlled style associated with the aristocracy.

By 1492—when Christopher Columbus was setting sail for America—the Spanish royals who had funded his journey, King Ferdinand and Queen Isabella, had finally regained control of their country with the defeat of the Moors in Granada, their last stronghold. Spain was about to enter its Golden Age, becoming for a time the most powerful country in the world. The wealth of the Spanish court, and the relative security of its people, meant more time for dancing and more inter-mingling of dances between classes.

COURTSHIP DANCES OF THE GOLDEN AGE

The dances seen during Spain's Golden Age (sixteenth and seventeenth centuries), by and large, were couple dances. The oldest of these is probably the *seguidilla*, a courtship song and dance that featured small springing steps and light foot stomps performed in a proud, almost taunting manner with partners using castanets and changing places throughout the song.

Like many Spanish dances, the song structure of the segui-dilla consisted of *coplas*—verses that were improvised by the singer on the spot, but which had a defined pattern of syllables, rhymes, and accents. For example, the seguidilla consisted of four coplas, each made up of four lines: seven syllables, then five, then seven, then five. As if that weren't challenging enough, the second and fourth lines had to rhyme. Dancing the seguidilla proved easier than singing it.

Many regions of Spain had their own version of the segui-dilla, the most popular being Seville's, which was called the *seguidillas sevillanas*, or *sevillanas* for short. This became the regional dance of Seville and is still known as "the mother of Spanish dance." Students at dance academies found it the first lesson on their syllabus. The sevillanas begins with an instrumental introduction followed by a section that is sung before the dancing begins. In between coplas, the dancers stop suddenly, holding their poses for an instrumental interlude before the next copla begins. The steps usually increase in difficulty and complexity as the coplas progress.

Another courtship dance that used coplas was the *jota*, from the province of Aragon. The jota may have originated as a fertility dance, though according to legend it was brought to Aragon by a Moorish poet named Aben Jot. In it, the couple hold their arms high over their heads while clicking castanets and leaping to the strains of the guitar.

Closely related to the jota and the sevillanas is the *fandango*, yet another courtship dance that probably originated with the Moors but which reached the height of its popularity in the 1700s and is still danced today. The fandango starts out slowly, the dancers clapping, snapping their fingers, stamping their feet, and clicking their castanets to the rhythm as it gradually increases in tempo. The man and woman pursue and retreat from one another, teasing and challenging the other, never letting any parts of their bodies touch. At the height of the music, when both musicians and dancers have reached a fever pitch, the music suddenly stops and the dancers freeze, holding their positions rigidly for a long pause before the music resumes.

The fiery fandango inspired passion in both dancers and spectators, as its repetitive buildup of movement and emotion seemed to portray the pacing and intensity of romantic love. In fact, when the famous seducer Giovanni Giacomo Casanova first saw it danced in 1767, he wrote: "They take a thousand attitudes, make a thousand gestures so lascivious that nothing can compare with them. This dance is the expression of love from beginning to end, from the sigh of desire to the ecstasy of enjoyment. It seemed to me impossible that after such a dance the girl could refuse anything to her partner."[6]

THE BOLERO AND ESCUELA BOLERA

Over the course of the eighteenth century, Spain's power had declined as she competed with Britain and France for colonial rights in the Americas. In the second half of the century, as the modernizing forces of the European Enlightenment swirled around Spain, a nationalistic feeling arose in the upper and middle classes, which embraced all things native and eschewed the tendency of some to admire or imitate the customs of France and other foreigners.

About this time, between 1750 and 1780, a new dance called the *bolero* was created, a solo or couple dance based on a modified, more elaborate version of the seguidillas. To the accompaniment of guitars, tambourines, and castanets, the bolero dancer combined brilliant and intricate movements from several other dances, including: a rhythmic introductory walk, various beating steps, and, like the sevillanas and fandango, a sudden stop. As time went by, the tempo of the bolero eventually slowed down. A good orchestral example of its song structure is Maurice Ravel's "Boléro."

The bolero soon made its way into ballrooms and onto stages as a truly Spanish dance that could compete with the popular French imports like minuets, contradanses, and ballet. Professional bolero dancers and dancing masters abounded and were not limited to the upper classes; even villagers wanted to learn the dance in order to perform it in taverns.

This led in the early 1800s to the genre known as *escuela bolera*, a theatrical form of dance that combined the bolero with other Spanish dances and elements of ballet into a codified system of Spanish classical dance.

Throughout the 1800s, when the rest of Europe was enthralled with the classical ballet that had come out of France and Italy, Spain proved to be the exception, holding instead to its own traditional dances, which emphasized much freer and more exotic range of movement in the torso and arms, livelier

While the rest of Europe adopted ballet in the 1800s, Spain created its own version of classical dance that mixed elements of ballet with native movements called *escuela bolera*.

and earthier footwork, and often loud stomps instead of the delicate pointe work of classical ballet.

As a result, many famous ballet masters and dancers borrowed from the Spanish repertoire. French dancer Armand Vestris danced the bolero in London; ballet masters such as Marius Petipa and August Bournonville studied Spanish dances and created Spanish ballets such as *El Toreador*, and renowned ballerinas such as Fanny Elssler experimented with the Spanish genre, winning over audiences worldwide.

Today the escuela bolera is taught alongside ballet in Spain's dance academies thanks in large part to one man, Angel Pericet Carmona, who in the early 1900s founded schools of Spanish dance first in Seville and later in Madrid. Carmona added more balletic elements to escuela bolera, such as soft ballet shoes, and wrote a manual codifying bolero steps and teaching instructions. Today five of his grandchildren carry on his work.

8

The Origins
of Flamenco

Flamenco, a style of music, song, and dance from the southern part of Spain called Andalusia, is an invention of the Gypsies who have been living in the region for centuries. *Flamenco* dancing consists of pounding, often frenzied footwork (*zapateado*) along with sinuous, florid movements of the arms (*braceo*) and hands (*florea*). It is usually a solo dance accompanied by a guitarist and sometimes a singer. Flamenco music and song are art forms unto themselves and are often performed without any dancing.

Flamenco remains a personal and intense form of dancing which—unlike many of the other dances described throughout this book—can still retain its original ritualistic powers: one of storytelling with the body, of catharsis, of pure emotional communication between dancer and onlooker, and even that of trance. But to begin to understand flamenco, one must first understand its Gypsy origins.

Flamenco is an organic expression of the dancer's emotion. Originating in the southern part of Spain known as Andalusia, *flamenco* emphasizes frenzied footwork and sinuous, florid movements of the arms.

THE GYPSIES

Sometime between the eighth and ninth centuries, hundreds of thousands of people living in northwestern India began migrating westward—no one is certain why. What is known is that one band of them traveled a northern route into south-eastern and eventually western Europe; today they are called Roma. Another branch took a southern route through Persia (Iran), Egypt, and North Africa, eventually arriving in southern Spain sometime between the ninth and fourteenth centuries. These Spanish Gypsies call themselves Gitano.

Some theorize that the Gypsies must have left India because they were one of the untouchable Hindu castes, people excluded from society based on conditions of their birth or on certain jobs they held. This seems to be supported by the work Gypsies undertook once in Spain: animal training and trading, metalworking, dancing, and palmistry. They brought musical instruments with them such as bells, tambourines, and wooden castanets, along with many songs and dances.

Whenever the Gypsies arrived in Andalusia, one thing is certain: It was still under Moorish (African Muslim) control. The Moors had rich musical and dance traditions, and these of course mixed with the Gypsies' own style over the centuries. For instance, the Moors' five-string lute could be the precursor to the Gypsies' flamenco guitar, and the melancholy, wailing sounds of the flamenco singer have been compared to the Muslim call to prayer. Flamenco's emphasis on the curving and articulated movements of the torso, arms, and hands also bears similarities to Indian dance.

The Gypsies have had a long history of persecution in the countries in which they eventually settled, and Spain was no different. They had several things working against them: they were foreigners, intermittently nomadic, and tended to stay outside the mainstream, preferring their own clan, keeping to their own language and customs, and displaying a strong sense of familial pride. In short, they weren't an easily con-trollable population.

So when King Ferdinand and Queen Isabella finally won Spain back from the Moors in 1492 and began the Spanish

Inquisition in an attempt to rid the country of non-Christians and foreign influence, the Gypsies didn't fare well. Their dress and language were banned, they were forbidden to travel in groups larger than two, and they were forced into ghettos in the southern cities of Seville, Cadiz, Jerez, and Granada, where they remained for three hundred years. It was in these ghettos, called *gitanerias*, that flamenco was probably born, a private expression of the Gypsies' longing and suffering, performed round a campfire in the hills outside of town where they lived—a lone man singing, another playing guitar, and perhaps one woman dancing as their families looked on, clapping and shouting.

Flamenco was also danced at Gypsy weddings, funerals, and baptisms, lending itself to happy occasions as well as mournful ones. But until the late eighteenth century, no one outside of the gitanerias was aware of it; it remained a purely Gypsy ritual.

Then, in 1782, King Charles III issued a series of domestic reforms, one of which, the Leniency Edict, restored some rights to Gypsies, allowing them to settle and work where they liked and to become more accepted into Spanish society. For the first time, the world outside the gitanerias got a glimpse of flamenco.

DUENDE: THE SPIRIT OF FLAMENCO

Ask what is meant by duende, and the answers will vary. Some will say it is the spirit that moves behind all flamenco, an outside force that enters a singer or dancer—perhaps even the spirit of a Gypsy ancestor—one that is called up by the flamenco the way spirits are summoned during a séance. Others will say it is the dancer's ability to expose his or her soul through the dance. Still others call duende a trance, a magical state of consciousness typically entered by the dancer after about fifteen minutes of rapid, focused zapateado, when the lips quiver, the eyes close, sweat streams down the face, and the dancer seems to be elsewhere, connected to some fountain of emotion deep inside herself.

What is clear is that flamenco was and is a ritual dance. Though it can be danced for pure enjoyment, for entertainment, or even for social reasons, its primary goal is an emotional and spiritual one: to transport both dancer and *palmeros*— onlookers who participate by clapping out the rhythm and shouting their approval—into an altered state of consciousness, connecting all of them to a source of passionate intensity deep within themselves.

The essence of flamenco is sorrow. There are dozens of types of dances in the flamenco repertoire—some more lighthearted than others—but in all there is an underlying sense of loss that makes the sad dances even sadder and the happy ones bittersweet. The lighthearted dances, called *cantes chicos* (light song), are more melodic and somewhat easier to perform. The heavier dances, *cantes jondos* (deep song), are the heart of flamenco. They are sung in rough, low, often hoarse voices with a sense of inner tension. Often singers' faces contort as if in pain as they hold a note, experimenting with all the tones and scales within it in a way that sounds very much like Middle-Eastern chanting. The flamenco songs portray simple lyrics of suffering, persecution, the cruelty of fate, and the pain of love.

"If I could pour all my pain
Into the streams
The water in the sea
Would rise to the heavens."[7]

But these are not whimpering songs; they are sung, and danced, with a stoic sense of pride and fiery passion. Flamenco is intimately linked to the Andalusion tradition of bullfighting, and a flamenco dancer resembles a bullfighter who is dancing with life—and death—itself, leaning, spinning, and pushing

Flamenco was first danced solely at Gypsy family gatherings before moving to cafés and theaters. Here a group of Gypsies from Granada, in southern Spain, dance the *flamenco*.

the torso up and the chest out wide as if facing down some invisible enemy.

Although it can be danced by a group, flamenco was meant as a solo because of its introverted and intimate nature. Flamenco dances were never choreographed with a set pattern of steps the way other folk dances were; instead, dancers learned some basic patterns, but were expected to piece these together into their own individual puzzle, improvising according to how the spirit moved them. Flamenco guitarists often followed the dancers, letting the dancer's improvisations lead the way through the music. This improvised structure meant that each time dancers got up to perform, they were using their bodies to tell their own story, letting onlookers look into their souls. It also made each performance completely unique.

The direction of flamenco is downward, into the earth. Though the arms make fanciful patterns above the head, the gaze is often cast downward as the legs pound the floor, pushing the physical and emotional energy out of the body through the feet. In this way, it is the opposite of more acrobatic and classical forms of dance, such as ballet, which movements center around rising as far off the ground as possible; to appear weightless.

THE CAFÉS CANTANTES

When flamenco emerged from the gitanerias in the early nine-teenth century, it entered what scholars call a "golden age," as singers and dancers took it public. The venues where it flour-ished were small cafés throughout southern Spain called *cafés cantantes* where patrons could sit and drink while watching flamenco danced on a *tablao* (platform). The first such café, Café sin Nombre (No Name Café), was opened by Silverio Franconetti in Seville in 1842.

The café cantantes, of course, altered the way flamenco was traditionally danced. While men were previously the sole singers and women the sole dancers, the cafés afforded both genders a chance to dance, though the men's style differed in that their zapateado was more pronounced, while their arms were held straighter than the women's.

Castanets weren't originally part of flamenco dance, as the hands had to remain free to clap and snap fingers, but in the cafés castanets became more common, adding another layer of percussion to the foot stomping.

While men wore dark trousers, white shirts, and cummer-bunds, sometimes with short bolero jackets similar to bullfighters', the women began to wear flounced gowns with long trains known as *batas de colas*. They could maneuver the trains of the gowns in much the same way a bullfighter would brandish his cape. In addition to emphasizing the woman's figure, the

Flamenco cafés, or *cafés cantantes*, popularized the dance form in the nineteenth and twentieth centuries. Patrons at the cafés could sit and drink while watching the *flamenco* performed on a *tablao* (platform).

gowns made for a prop to be manipulated during the dance as the woman swished and spun quickly in place, the long train trailing behind and around her. Unlike many other forms of dance, the female flamenco dancer didn't necessarily have to be young, slim, or traditionally beautiful; older women could dance it with just as much feeling and often more mastery.

The main advantage of the cafés, of course, was that Gypsies could earn a livelihood from their dancing.

The cafés made flamenco wildly popular, and soon it was transformed from an intimate experience into a stage art replete with other dances from the escuela bolera. In 1862, the first flamenco performance for tourists was staged in Granada, and in 1866 the same happened in Seville. The cafés cantantes continued to proliferate until the 1920s.

THE DECLINE OF PURE FLAMENCO

If the cafés cantantes bolstered the art of flamenco while keeping its basic structure and focus intact, the next stage in the evolution of flamenco distorted it until it was barely recognized as the art form the Gypsies had handed down a century earlier.

In the late 1800s and early 1900s, flamenco made its way from the cafés of Andalusia to the music hall stages of Madrid, Barcelona, and other large cities in Europe and South America. This is a classic example of an ethnic or ritualistic dance that has been taken out of its original context, but in this case nearly all was lost in the translation.

The introverted, intimate nuances of the dance were lost on the larger stage. The dancers, mostly women by this time, were moved to the front of the stage, further away from the singers and musicians, who took a back seat to the dance instead of playing their traditional equal roles. The singing became lighter and higher-pitched, a style that has been referred to as "operatic flamenco," which meant that the songs' gravelly and earthy wails no longer aroused the same emotions in the audience or the dancers. In fact, the whole enterprise began to take on the comical tone of a variety show. There could be as many as twenty dances shown in an evening, between which men dressed as women would perform comedic songs or a Charlie Chaplin film would be shown.

Flamenco was wildly popular, but it wasn't exactly flamenco anymore. However, that was about to change, thanks to a young girl who had recently given up classical dance to learn flamenco, and to an Andalusian poet who made it his aim to revitalize authentic Spanish poetry, theatre, and dance—including the earlier form of flamenco danced by the Gypsies, for whom he held a particular admiration.

9

Flamenco in the Twentieth Century

THE "FLAMENCO PAVLOVA"

Antonia Mercé was born in Buenos Aires, Argentina, but both her parents were Spanish, and both were professional dancers. They returned with her to Spain when she was only two years old, and her father, highly skilled in both ballet and escuela bolera, taught her these classical forms of dance. She must have been a born dancer, for she made her debut at six years of age, and by the time she was eleven had already been promoted to the rank of soloist at the company of the Madrid Opera.

But at the tender age of fourteen, Mercé decided she was more interested in Spanish folk dances and in flamenco than in escuela bolera. So she "resigned" from the Madrid Opera and began to study flamenco in Andalusia, working at cafés cantantes, in *peñas* (flamenco bars), and seeking out elderly Gypsy women who could teach her the art of zapateado and

Antonia Mercé, or "La Argentina," was schooled in classical dance but devoted her career to traditional *flamenco*. Her world tours spawned the *flamenco* revival of the early 1900s.

florea. After four years of intensive training, she began to tour under the stage name "La Argentina."

Possessing of a brilliant natural sense of timing and especially skilled in castanet playing, La Argentina eventually became the world's foremost Spanish dancer, touring throughout Europe and later throughout the world. Her early classical training, combined with her intense study of flamenco and her natural gifts, made her technique more integrated and polished than had previously been seen on the stage. She also helped elevate the status of flamenco onto a level on par with the classical escuela bolera, and to gain for it worldwide familiarity and respect. Her constant touring made her known as the "Flamenco Pavlova," a comparison to the ballerina Anna Pavlova who was bringing knowledge of classical ballet to the world around the same time.

By 1928, La Argentina had formed her own company and had a repertoire of sixty-seven solo dances she presented on tours. While La Argentina's style was "bigger" and covered a larger floor space than traditional flamenco had in the crowded cafés of Andalusia, she nevertheless preserved much of the beauty, intensity, and emotion of the dance. That is why many critics and scholars agree that La Argentina played a vital role in the rebirth of flamenco that occurred during this time, spawning not only many devoted aficionados but also the careers of other dancers who would go on to pass down the flamenco tradition, keeping it alive to the present day.

LORCA, FALLA, AND FLAMENCO'S REBIRTH

Another person who figured prominently in flamenco's neo-classical period was Federico Garcia Lorca, a poet and playwright born in Granada in 1888—the same year that La Argentina was born in Buenos Aires. Lorca decried the commercialization and distortion of flamenco that was taking place in concert halls in the early twentieth century. He and other Spanish intellectuals, including the composer Manual de Falla, attempted to rescue the legacy of authentic flamenco for future generations.

In 1915, Falla distilled old Andalusian folk rhythms into a score for a ballet based on a Gypsy legend called *El Amor Brujo (Love, the Sorcerer)*. Ten years later, La Argentina did the chore-ography, making *El Amor* famous with her "Ritual Fire Dance" and "Dance of Terror." Then in 1922, Falla and Garcia Lorca organized the first-ever flamenco competition in Granada, which drew Gypsies from all over southern Spain to compete in singing and dancing "primitive Andalusian" songs.

Carmen Amaya was one of a handful of flamenco dancers who kept the tradition alive during the twentieth century. Following in the footsteps of "La Argentina," Amaya focused on the elements of pure dance instead of plot and scenery.

In the 1920s, Lorca published *The Gypsy Ballads*, poems in which he tried to capture the trancelike power of flamenco and what he called its "dark sounds." In fact, Lorca devoted much of his time attempting to communicate the experience of duende.

Meanwhile, dancers such as Carmen Amaya, Vicente Escudero, José Greco, and Pilar Lopez were following in La Argentina's footsteps as practitioners of neoclassical Spanish dance. Though by this time many of them were developing longer and longer dances and even creating full-length flamenco ballets, Amaya in particular kept the elements of plot and scenery out of the picture, focusing instead on the pure dance. Lopez and Greco created their own company, Ballet Espagnol, and went on to train a new generation of mostly male dancers who are still alive today, such as Antonio Gades and Manolo Vargas.

As usual, political events affected these cultural efforts. In 1936, rebels who called themselves Nationalists, and who were backed by the German Nazis and the Italian Fascists, attempted a military coup to take control of Spain's Republican government. When that failed, the bloody Spanish Civil War broke out. In three years, it would claim the lives of half a million Spaniards, leaving fascist dictator Francisco Franco in control of the country, Garcia Lorca executed for his liberal views (as well as his homosexuality), and Spain isolated from the rest of the Western world.

FLAMENCO TODAY

Franco ruled Spain until his death in 1975, and a few years later Spain was restored to a democratic constitutional monarchy. But even with Spain's relative seclusion during the reign of Franco, the world didn't forget about flamenco. The tradition was kept alive in the United States by several teachers such as Carola Goya, Matteo Marcellus Vittuci, Teo Morca, and Maria Benitez. As the United States Hispanic population grew, so did flamenco's appeal.

But flamenco certainly enjoyed a revival of sorts in the years after Franco's death. This was spurred by the founding of two national dance companies by the Spanish Ministry of Culture—the Ballet Nacional Espanol and the Ballet Nacional Classico. In addition, one of Lorca's Gypsy plays, *Blood Wedding*, was made into a flamenco ballet by Antonio Gades and later translated to film by director Carlos Saura. Saura's trilogy of flamenco films in the 1980s—*Blood Wedding*, *Carmen*, and *El Amor Brujo*—reacquainted viewers around the world with the genre.

Today flamenco is more popular than ever, though its popular form has definitely merged with other dance genres such as ballet and escuela bolera—as well as with theatrical elements such as plot, scenery, and nontraditional costumes—to create a modern kind of flamenco fusion. The modern flamenco dancer is younger and more athletic than the Gypsies of old. He can play castanets and execute rapid zapateado, yet also spin, jump, and act. Stars such as Joaquin Cortes, Sara Baras, and Antonio Canales play to sold-out audiences worldwide. Flamenco has gained a wide following in Australia, England, Japan, Sweden, France, and Israel as well as the United States.

Flamenco, like so many of the dances described in this book, started as a ritualistic, even magical means of expression by a tight-knit ethnic group, a way for them to communicate the important events and passions of their lives. Just like the Irish reel and the Polish chodzony, once it was seen by a large number of people, it spread fast and quickly changed form. It became less ritualistic and more entertainment-oriented, then professional, and even theatrical. Later, it was given classical treatment by a group of well-trained dancers and made accessible to the masses. All of this took flamenco far afield of its origins in the Gypsy ghettos and cafés of Andalusia.

It seems as though any type of dance, once it's "out of its cage," so to speak, is bound to keep changing as it spreads throughout a culture—which today means a global culture—merging with other forms and continually evolving.

However, unlike most other dance, flamenco still retains much of its ritualistic dimensions. It should come as no surprise that the place to experience this firsthand is Andalusia, where dancers and audiences relive the intimate setting of the cafés cantantes in modern-day clubs called *tablaos*, where Gypsies still live and dance flamenco to celebrate life's passages, and where, in the company of a skilled dancer, one can still experience the magic of duende.

A GYPSY FIESTA

Although worldwide sensations such as Cumbre Flamenca display a modern, virtuosic kind of flamenco, we can enter the world where flamenco was born, and see how it is still practiced, via the 2000 Spanish documentary *Heritage of Flamenco*. In it, a large Gypsy clan is enjoying a fiesta.

People of all ages sit in chairs in a circle, surrounded by tables holding bottles of wine. The men are dressed in suits and the women wear dresses or skirts with long scarves around their necks. Two young men play guitars; between them a dark-haired woman of about sixty years old is singing. Her voice is rough and hoarse, but it holds the melody stubbornly, twisting the last notes of each phrase into an Islamic-sounding wail as her eyes squint shut and her hands come up to her face. Between verses, the guitars play and she looks toward them, keeping time with the rest of the family, who are all clapping and stomping their feet to the rhythm, shouting "olé!"

As the long song goes on, one by one people rise from their chairs, move to the middle of the floor and begin their solo dances. The first is an old but trim man, his face still handsome, dressed in a gray suit. As he walks to the middle of the room, his arms slowly lift up and away from his body, as if a wind were gathering under him. His fingers snap in time to the music until his hands are above his head.

When he reaches the center, arms still high above him, he begins stomping his feet exactly as a bullfighter would, ending each round of stomps with a quick spin and then snapping his feet together as his arms whip around his waist. He uses the tails of his coat jacket as if they are a matador's cape, holding them out, then dropping his palms to hit his thighs before letting his arms fly up again. Each time he pulls his body and arms upward, it looks as if he is actually trying to escape something that is stampeding right by him. Soon one shoulder of his jacket comes off, then another. Then, still stomping his feet as the palmeros cry "olé," he ties the ends of his shirt into a knot, swerving his hips right and left while his hands frame his head in fanciful patterns of curlicues.

A young man rises to dance, perhaps seventeen years old. His long black hair hangs in his eyes and he is wearing a tan suit and cowboy boots. He stands quietly in the center of the room, arms raised, awaiting the right musical cue. Then he begins a rapid series of heel-and-toe stomps that look identical to the kind performed by Michael Flatley in *Lord of the Dance*—except faster. Every now and then his heels fly up in back and he hits them with the opposite hand. The angle of the dance is a continuous series of oppositions. If the feet are pounding heavily the torso is lifted up and away, and if the torso is leaning right the head is looking left. The boy slaps his thighs and finishes his footwork in a series so rapid it becomes a blur.

Later, at a party inside a cave that has been painted white and decorated with colorful wall hangings, a smaller group of Gypsies sit drinking and clapping in time to a flamenco guitar and singer. A heavy, middle-aged woman with shiny black hair pulled tightly away from her face gets up, smiling. She hikes her full black skirt up to her thighs and begins to wildly pound the floor with her feet, twisting her head violently right, then left with her eyes closed. Continuing her footwork, her arms begin curling up both sides of her body, the wrists and fingers moving ceaselessly, like a frilly curtain being raised on a piece of artwork. Once above her head, her hands keep tracing intricate patterns in the air, her feet moving faster and faster. Suddenly she looks down, spins in place, and in one rapid *swoosh* lands on the floor, knees bent and splayed out with her skirt gathered between them and her back flat on the floor. Then slowly her hands lift away from her prone body, her wrists curling around and around, and gradually she lifts her torso off the floor until she is kneeling straight up on her knees. With another spin she's up and standing, stomping across the room straight to her chair, where she falls laughing as the music ends on the very same note.

Andalusia The southern part of Spain where Gypsies developed flamenco dancing.

baile The Spanish term for common dancing that is earthy and lively.

batas de colas A dress with a long ruffled train, worn by female flamenco dancers.

bolero A lively Spanish dance originating in the eighteenth century, in which dancers perform intricate steps involving battements (beating of the feet) and sudden stops, while playing castanets.

braceo The graceful, curving arm work used in flamenco dancing.

British Isles The islands of Great Britain, Ireland, and many smaller surrounding islands.

cafés cantante A type of nineteenth-century Spanish café that became the setting for flamenco musicians, dancers, and singers to show their craft.

cake dance An old Irish dance performed near alehouses, for which the prize was a cake.

cantes chico Translates to "light song," a type of flamenco song (and dance) that is simpler in rhythm and more lighthearted in tone than *cantes jondo.*

cantes jondo Translates to "deep song," a type of flamenco song (and dance) with a complex, twelve-beat structure and profound, often sorrowful themes of suffering, despair, and death.

castanets Small hand instruments made of either shell, wood, or ivory and used by the dancer as percussion accompaniment.

ceili An Irish social dance in which participants do standardized and relatively simple dances such as the eight-hand reel and High Caul Cap in groups.

Celts The ancient tribe of people who eventually settled in many parts of Europe, including Ireland and southern Spain, and who are the direct ancestors of today's Irish.

chodzony An old Polish walking dance, performed in village processions, which eventually developed into the *polonez*.

Connemara A rugged coastal and island region of western Ireland where old-style, or *sean-nos*, dancing is still practiced.

coplas In Spanish song and dance, a verse or stanza of the song.

country dance See *set dance*.

country set See *set dance*.

danza (1) The Spanish term for dancing that is controlled, refined, and practiced more by professionals and, in previous centuries, by the upper classes. (2) Religiously themed dances sponsored by the Catholic Church in twelfth and thirteenth century Spain.

duende Literally "goblin" or "elf," the term used by flamenco dancers to describe the trancelike state of profound emotion that can be attained after many minutes of intensely focused flamenco dancing.

escuela bolera The genre of Spanish classical dancing developed in the nineteenth century that combines the *bolero* with other Spanish dance steps as well as ballet to create a uniquely Spanish form of academic dance.

ethnic dance A term used to describe dances done by a particular ethnic group spontaneously and usually for ritualistic reasons, as opposed to *social dance, theatrical dance,* or *competitive dance.* Although they are not completely synonymous, ethnic dance is commonly called *folk dance.*

Falla, Manual de Spanish composer who wrote the music for the flamenco ballets *El Amor Brujo* and *El Sombrero de Tres Picos* (The Three Cornered Hat), and who along with Garcia Lorca organized the first flamenco competition in 1922.

figures Refers to the patterns a group of dancers trace on the floor, such as figure-eights, squares, circles, or lines, as opposed to the actual steps or footwork the dancers perform while making the figures.

flamenco The ethnic music, song, and dance of Gypsies living in Andalusia. Dance-wise, flamenco combines percussive footwork with intricate use of the hands, torso, and arms.

florea In flamenco dancing, the complex and florid use of the hands, especially performed by women.

folk dance A more common and broader term for *ethnic dance,* folk dance typically refers to a dance that originated as a ritualistic or celebratory function of a particular ethnic group but today might be revived outside its original context either as a performance, in a competition, or in a social setting (see *social dance*).

Gaelic League An organization founded in the late 1800s to preserve and revive traditional Irish (Gaelic) language and culture.

Great Britain Refers to the countries of England, Scotland, and Wales, all located on the same island off the northwestern coast of Europe.

Gypsies A tribe originally from northwestern India who began migrating west in the eighth and ninth centuries, eventually settling in several European countries where they are known as Rom or Roma, and also in southern Spain where they refer to themselves as Gitano.

half-set A **set dance** similar to the *quadrille* but involving two couples instead of four.

hornpipe One of the oldest dances of the British Isles; today in Ireland the hornpipe is a complex and difficult *step dance* performed to relatively slow music.

Iberian Peninsula The large peninsula in southwestern Europe that contains Spain and Portugal and that is bounded on three sides by the Atlantic Ocean and the Mediterranean Sea.

Irish Republic The independent Irish state comprised of twenty-six southern counties on the island of Ireland. The republic shares the island with Northern Ireland.

jig (1) A fast Irish step dance performed either as a solo or in groups or couples. (2) Can also refer to any solo step dance done to jig-time music.

krakowiak One of five national Polish dances, the krakowiak is a fast and lively dance for many couples that features a basic galloping step along with foot stomps and heel clicks.

kujawiak One of five national Polish dances, the kujawiak is a lyrical, romantic dance for couples that often features three parts: a processional or simple walking introduction, a middle section of slow graceful turns, and a lively ending full of fast spinning.

La Argentina see *Mercé, Antonia*.

long dance An old dance in many parts of Europe involving two lines of dancers, one of men and one of women.

Lorca, Federico Garcia Spanish poet and playwright who helped usher in a rebirth of *flamenco* with his poems, including *The Gypsy Ballads*, his play *Blood Wedding*, and his organization of the first-ever flamenco competition in 1922.

Malopolska or **Lesser Poland** The region in southeastern Poland where the Carpathian Mountains lie and many diverse ethnic groups live.

Mazovia A region in central eastern Poland that contains Warsaw.

mazur One of Poland's five national dances, the mazur originated in the sixteenth century. It features a smooth running step punctuated by slight hops, heel clicks, and foot stamps, and very fast turns. Throughout Europe it became known as the mazurka.

Mazuria The region of northeastern Poland where the *mazur* comes from.

Mercé, Antonia Brilliant Spanish and flamenco dancer of the early twentieth century whose tours helped spread flamenco around the world.

Middle Ages The period between about 400–1200 A.D. after the fall of the Roman Empire when much of Europe's infrastructure collapsed, various armies invaded, feudalism took root, and art, science, and culture went into a period of stagnation.

Moors North-African Muslims who invaded Spain and fought Christians for control of it from the eighth to the fifteenth centuries.

morisca A Spanish dance that portrays a mock battle between Christians and the Moors.

morris dance A ceremonial English dance performed usually by men in two long lines.

Munster The region of southwestern Ireland associated with the standard style of step dancing seen today.

Northern Ireland The six counties that comprise the northernmost tip of the island of Ireland, which are part of the United Kingdom along with Great Britain.

oberek One of Poland's five national dances, the oberek is a fast and improvisational dance for couples which features acrobatic feats by the men. It can also be called the *oberta*.

palmeros Onlookers who participate in flamenco dance and song by clapping out the rhythm and shouting encouragement.

polka A dance that originated in the Czech Republic, migrated throughout Europe in the nineteenth century, and is now performed in a modified version mostly by Polish- and German-American immigrants and their descendants. Its basic structure is a hop and three steps performed while turning as a couple.

polonez One of Poland's five national dances, the polonez is a slow, simple walking processional for couples that features long bows between verses. It is also known as the *polonaise*.

Pomerania The region of northwestern Poland bordering the Baltic Sea.

promenade A basic Irish step, similar to the side step, in which the dancer hops and takes three steps to either the right or left all on the ball of the feet.

quadrille A French ballroom dance for four couples in a square formation, the quadrille became one of the most popular European dances of the nineteenth century.

reel (1) A dance in which two or more couples alternate steps in place with traveling moves. In Ireland, a reel is often performed as a solo step dance similar to a *jig*. (2) Can also refer to any Irish step dance done to reel-time music.

rince fada The Gaelic term for a long dance.

rising step The basic step of the *Irish jig*, in which the dancer brushes the front knee to the back and transfers the weight between the feet, all on the balls of the feet.

round dance Any variety of old ethnic dances involving people moving in a circle, usually around a tree, fire, or symbolic object.

Saura, Carlos Spanish film director known for his trilogy of flamenco dance-dramas: *Blood Wedding, Carmen,* and *El Amor Brujo.*

sean-nos In Gaelic, "old-style," it refers to the traditional style of step dancing that is heavier, more flat-footed, and improvisational as opposed to airborne and athletic.

seguidilla An old Spanish courtship dance that features small springing steps and light foot stomps performed in a proud, taunting manner with partners using castanets and changing places throughout the song.

set dance A type of social dance popular in much of Europe from the sixteenth century to the present. In it, couples move in circles, lines, or squares to standard or "set" steps. Also called a *country dance* or a *country set*. The most popular set dance was the *quadrille,* a French dance involving four couples which, when imported to Ireland, was sometimes simply called a *set.*

sevillanas Short for *seguidilla sevillana,* a *seguidilla* from the region of Seville that increases in difficulty as the music progresses and features many sudden stops.

side step The basic step of the Irish reel, in which the dancer hops and takes six steps to the right or left on the balls of the feet.

Silesia The southwestern region of Poland bordering the Czech Republic.

Slavs A tribe who migrated from Asia to Europe in the third millennium B.C. The western branch of this tribe today inhabits Poland, the Czech Republic, Slovakia, Belarus, Ukraine, Russia, Serbia, Croatia, Slovenia, Bosnia, and Montenegro.

sink and **grind** A basic Irish step in which the dancer jumps on both feet, brushes the leg to the front then back, then transfers the weight between the feet.

social dance A dance performed mainly for social enjoyment as opposed to ritual, performance, or competition.

step dance A type of Irish dance that features complicated footwork and a rigid torso and arms; step dance can be performed as a solo or as part of a group dance.

sword dance A very old type of dance in many cultures around the world which may be left over from ancient war dances, and which features men hitting sticks or swords together or forming complex arrangements with them.

tablaos In flamenco dancing, (1) a raised platform usually in a bar where patrons could watch a dancer perform. (2) a modern-day Spanish club for flamenco dancing and singing.

theatrical dance Dance that is performed mainly for dramatic purposes, to a passive audience, and usually involving theatrical elements such as plot and scenery.

traditional dance Another term for folk dance.

two short threes A basic Irish step in which the dancer hops and flips the front leg to the back with bent knee first on the right, then the left.

Ulster The northernmost region of Ireland, which today is virtually synonymous with Northern Ireland.

United Kingdom The nation formed by England, Wales, and Scotland (Great Britain) plus Northern Ireland.

waltz A triple-time dance for couples that originated in Austria and became popular throughout Europe in the eighteenth century.

Wielkopolska or **Greater Poland** The central western region of Poland.

zapateado The element of flamenco dancing emphasizing percussive, fast footwork.

zbojnicki or **hatchet dance** An energetic circular dance where men of the Tatra Mountains in southern Poland carry hatchets, sing, and leap high into the air.

	IRELAND	POLAND	SPAIN
700s B.C.			Celts arrive in Spain, joining Iberians.
300s B.C.	Celts arrive.		
200s B.C.			Rome conquers Spain.
400s A.D.	St. Patrick brings Christianity to Ireland.	Slavs arrive in Poland and Eastern Europe.	
500s			Catholicism becomes Spain's official religion.
700s			Moors invade Spain.
800s			Earliest date Gypsies may have arrived in Andalusia.
900s		First Polish kingdom established.	
1100s	Anglo-Normans invade. *Round dances* seen.		*Morisca* danced at royal wedding. Church sponsors *danzas* and *Los Seises*.
1300s		Poland unites with Lithuania, spawning Golden Age. Early *krakowiak* danced at weddings.	
1400s		*Chodzony* danced rurally.	Ferdinand and Isabella reconquer Spain from Moors; Inquisition begins; Gypsies forced into gitanerias.
1500s	*Hey* and *rince fada* danced by villagers.	*Polonez* danced at royal wedding. *Mazur* danced by Mazury tribe. Poland becomes an elected monarchy.	Spain's Golden Age.
1600s	*Withy dances*, *cake dances*, *sword dances*, and *reel* seen.	*Mazur* moves to the royal courts.	*Seguidillas* and *jota* widely danced.
1700s	Dancing masters teach *step dance*, *ceili dances*, and *set dances*. British sailors make *hornpipe* popular.	*Polonez* danced throughout Europe as *polonaise*. Poland loses sovereignty to its partitioners.	*Fandango* reaches peak of its popularity as a courtship dance. *Bolero* introduced. Charles III grants freedoms to Gypsies.
1800s	**1840s:** Potato famine. **1890s:** Gaelic League founded.	**1830s:** Ballerina Fanny Elssler makes *krakowiak* ("cracovienne") famous. **1840s:** *Polka* reaches height of popularity in Europe. *Oberek* danced. **1870s:** *Mazurka* seen in ballets *Swan Lake* and *Coppelia*.	*Escuela bolera* merges elements of *bolero* and other dances with *ballet*. **1840s:** *Flamenco* first seen in cafés cantantes. **1890s:** Angel Carmona Pericet founds school to teach *escuela bolera*.

106

	IRELAND	POLAND	SPAIN
1900			*Flamenco* moves into large music halls.
1910s		**1918**: Poland freed from partitioners' rule.	**1915**: Malla composes *El Amor Brujo*.
1920s	**1929**: Gaelic League publishes 30 standard ceili dances, founds step-dance schools.		**1922**: First *flamenco* competition in Andalusia. **1928**: Lorca publishes *The Gypsy Ballads*. La Argentina forms her own dance company.
1930s	**1930**: Irish Dancing Commission founded. **1936**: Public Halls Dance Act requires permits for holding dances. **1939**: First standard step-dance manuals published by Irish Dancing Commission.	**1930**: Scholars at Warsaw University begin studying Poland's folk dances. **1939**: Poland occupied by Germany and Russia during WWII.	**1936**: Spanish Civil War. **1939**: Fascist dictator Francisco Francocomes to power.
1940s		**1946**: Poland comes under Soviet Communist rule. **1947**: Balanchine ballet *Theme and Variations* features *polonez*. **1948**: Mazowsze Folk Dance Ensemble founded.	**1942**: Pericet publishes codified steps of *escuela bolero*.
1950s		**1953**: Slask Song and Dance Ensemble founded.	
1960s		**1968**: Institute of Art begins documenting folk dances.	
1970s	*Sean-nos* revival in Connemara.	**1978**: Cardinal Karol Wojtyla elected Pope John Paul II.	**1975**: Franco dies.
1980s	Set dancing revival.	**1989**: Freed from communist rule, becomes Republic of Poland	Carlos Saura directs trilogy of *flamenco* films: *Blood Wedding*, *El Amor Brujo*, and *Carmen*.
1990s	**1994**: *Riverdance* premieres.		

Videography

Ireland

Celtic Feet: Irish Dancing Step by Step. Acorn Media, 1996.

Lord of the Dance, directed by David Mallet. Universal Studios, 1997.

Riverdance: The Show, directed by John McClogan. Columbia/Tristar, 1995.

Poland

Mazowsze in Russia, 1999.

Pan Tadeusz, directed by Andrzej Wajda, 1999.

Slask: Songs and Dance by Slask, 1992.

Spain

Blood Wedding, directed by Carlos Saura. Xenon Studios, 1981.

El Amor Brujo (Love the Sorcerer), directed by Carlos Saura. Pacific Arts Video, 1992.

Flamenco, directed by Carlos Saura. New Yorker Films, 1997.

Sevillanas, directed by Carlos Saura. Connoisseur/Meridian Films, 1996.

www.folkdancing.org
By far the most comprehensive site on folk dancing in North America. Includes directories of more than three thousand folk dance groups and lessons listed by state; one thousand special events; and hundreds of articles on European and American folk dance.

Ireland
www.irelandsdance.com
The best site devoted solely to Irish step dancing, with history, photos, and a list of FAQs for beginners interested in pursuing *step dance.*

www.regorecords.com/rego/irishdance.html
The dance link of Rego Records' Website, with Irish dancing videos and Irish music available for sale.

Poland
www.poloniatoday.com
Online Polish-American magazine.

www.slask.art.pl
Official Website of the Slask Song and Dance Ensemble, one of Poland's most famous folk groups. Its Gallery link contains video clips of Slask performing a dozen Polish folk dances.

www.syrenadancers.com
Website of the Syrena Polish Folk Dance Ensemble of Milwaukee, Wisconsin, one of the leading folk troupes in the United States.

www.usc.edu/dept/polish_music/dance/dancelinks.html
Southern California has an active Polish folk dance community, and this list of links from the University of Southern California is comprehensive and worldwide.

Spain
www.flamencoshop.com
This site from Andalusia offers everything from articles on *flamenco*'s history to *flamenco* fashions to postcards.

www.flamencoworld.com
News, feature stories, music, and online video of current *flamenco* stars. A beautifully visual site that instantly communicates the look of modern *flamenco*.

Bennahum, Ninotchka. *Antonia Mercé "La Argentina": Flamenco and the Spanish Avant Garde.* Hanover, N.H.: Wesleyan University Press, 2000.

Brennan, Helen. *The Story of Irish Dance.* Lanham, Md.: Robert Rinehart Publishers, 1999.

Cahill, Thomas. *How the Irish Saved Civilization.* New York: Doubleday, 1995.

Cass, Joan. *Dancing Through History.* Englewood Cliffs, N.J.: Prentice Hall, 1993.

Craine, Debra and Judith Mackrell. *The Oxford Dictionary of Dance.* New York: Oxford University Press, 2000.

Dziewanowska, Ada. *Polish Folk Dances & Songs: A Step-by-Step Guide.* New York: Hippocrene Books, 1997.

Frazer, James. *The Golden Bough.* New York: Penguin Books, 1922.

Lawson, Joan. *European Folk Dance: Its National and Musical Characteristics.* London: Sir Isaac Pitman & Sons, 1953.

Schreiner, Claus (editor). *Flamenco: Gypsy Dance and Music From Andalusia.* Portland, Ore.: Amadeus Press, 1990.

Washabaugh, William. *Flamenco: Passion, Politics and Popular Culture.* Dulles, Va.: Berg, 1996.

Bennahum, Ninotchka. *Antonia Mercé "La Argentina": Flamenco and the Spanish Avant Garde.* Hanover, N.H.: Wesleyan University Press, 2000.

Dziewanowska, Ada. *Polish Folk Dances & Songs: A Step-by-Step Guide.* New York: Hippocrene Books, 1997.

Lorca, Federico Garcia. *In Search of Duende.* New York: New Directions, 1998.

Lorca, Federico Garcia. *Poem of the Deep Song (Poema del Cante Jondo).* San Francisco: City Lights Books, 1987.

Quinn, Tom. *Irish Dancing.* New York: Harper Collins, 1998.

Schafer, Andrea. *My Harvest Home: A Celebration of Polish Songs, Dances, Games & Customs* (book and CD). Danbury, Conn.: World Music Press, 1996.

Smyth, Sam. *Riverdance: The Story.* London: Trafalgar Square, 1997.

Webster, Jason. *Duende: A Journey Into the Heart of Flamenco.* New York: Broadway Books, 2002.

Notes

1 Helen Brennan. *The Story of Irish Dance.* Maryland: Roberts Rinehart Publishers, 1999. Page 18. (Originally Dineley, Thomas. *Voyage Through the Kingdom of Ireland in the Year 1841.* Dublin: M.H. Gill, 1870. Page 19.)

2 Brennan, Ibid. (Originally Head, Richard. *The Western Wonder,* 1670. Page 37.)

3 Frank Whelan. *The Complete Guide to Irish Dance.* Belfast: Appletree, 2000. Page 15.

4 Brennan, Page 34.

5 Brennan, Page 77.

6 Joan Cass. *Dancing Through History.* Englewood Cliffs, N.J.: Prentice Hall, 1993. Page 44.

7 Claus Schreiner (editor). *Flamenco: Gypsy Dance and Music From Andalusia.* Portland, Oregon: Amadeus Press, 1990. Page 22

Index

Index

Index

page:

13: Courtesy of The General Libraries, The University of Texas at Austin

17: © Hulton-Deutsch Collection/CORBIS

21: © Hulton|Archive by Getty Images

23: © Hulton|Archive by Getty Images

28: © Hulton|Archive by Getty Images

32: © Hulton|Archive by Getty Images

35: © Bettmann/CORBIS

39: AP/Wide World Photos

43: Courtesy of The General Libraries, The University of Texas at Austin

46: © PAGANI FLAVIO/CORBIS SYGMA

51: © Davis Lees/Time Life Pictures/ Getty Images

53: © Hulton|Archive by Getty Images

56: The J. Paul Getty Museum, Los Angeles © Courtesy of The J. Paul Getty Museum

60: © Julie Lemberger/CORBIS

63: © Hulton|Archive by Getty Images

67: AP/Wide World Photos

71: Courtesy of The General Libraries, The University of Texas at Austin

74: © Owen Franken/CORBIS

78: © Julie Lemberger/CORBIS

81: © Hulton|Archive by Getty Images

85: © Bettmann/CORBIS

87: © Paul Almasy/CORBIS

91: © Hulton|Archive by Getty Images

93: © Hulton|Archive by Getty Images

Cover: © Elke Stolzenberg/CORBIS
Frontis: © Hulton|Archive by Getty Images

About the Author

Robin Rinaldi has studied ballet, jazz, tap, modern, and Middle Eastern dance. A former technical writer, she has written more than 30 reference books, three of which won awards from the Northern California Society of Technical Writers. As a journalist, she has written dance reviews for the *Sacramento News & Review* and *Philadelphia Weekly*, interviewing such choreographers as Mark Morris, Ron Cunningham, David Parsons, and Judith Jamison. She lives in San Francisco, where she currently writes freelance magazine articles. She is also the author of *Ballet*, another volume in the WORLD OF DANCE series.